AF394771

LIFE.
RECLAIMED

LIFE. RECLAIMED

Find freedom from chronic overperformance

DR PIPPA GRANGE

TOP PERFORMANCE PSYCHOLOGIST

First published in Great Britain in 2026 by
DK RED, an imprint of Dorling Kindersley Limited
20 Vauxhall Bridge Road,
London SW1V 2SA

The authorised representative in the EEA is
Dorling Kindersley Verlag GmbH. Arnulfstr. 124, 80636 Munich, Germany

For all of the clients who taught me and teach me, still.

CONTENTS.

Introduction   13

Part 1: How We Learned Who to Be   27

Chapter 1: Stories the World Tells Us   31

Chapter 2: Stories You Tell Yourself   53

Chapter 3: Trauma and the Performer   71

Part 2: Overperformance and Its Consequences   89

Chapter 4: Ways We Overperform   93

Chapter 5: Crashing and Burning   113

Part 3: Crossing Thresholds   133

Chapter 6: Coming Home   137

Chapter 7: Getting Honest   153

Part 4: Regenerative Performance   173

Chapter 8: Better Reasons to Perform   177

Chapter 9: The Regenerative Performer   195

Final Word   223

Notes   225

Acknowledgements   233

All the True Vows

All the true vows
are secret vows,
the ones we speak out loud
are the ones we break.

There is only one life
you can call your own
and a thousand others
you can call by any name you want.

Hold to the truth you make
every day with your own body,
don't turn your face away.

Hold to your own truth
at the center of the image
you were born with.

Those who do not understand
their destiny, will never understand
the friends they have made,
nor the work they have chosen,

nor the one life that waits
beyond all the others.

By the lake in the wood,
in the shadows,
you can
whisper that truth
to the quiet reflection
you see in the water.

Whatever you hear from
the water, remember,

it wants you to carry
the sound of its truth on your lips.

Remember,
in this place
no one can hear you
and out of the silence
you can make a promise
it will kill you to break,

that way you'll find
what is real and what is not.

I know what I am saying.
Time almost forsook me
and I looked again.

Seeing my reflection
I broke a promise
and spoke
for the first time
after all these years

in my own voice

before it was too late
to turn my face again.

By David Whyte

INTRODUCTION

Have you ever wondered if you might be a bit addicted to pace and pressure? Do you regularly close off your feelings and ignore your body so that you can get more done? And is the internal narrator to your daily life critical of anything that doesn't add to your progress and betterment?

What if you could reclaim your life back from the pressure of a ticking clock and the external scoreboard? What if you could remember who you were before all that expectation?

This is a book for all you performers who try your heart out at this "humaning" thing and find yourself wiped out by tiredness and nagging doubt, wondering how to recalibrate and re-energise before you crash. Maybe it's time we talked about it.

As a performance psychologist, I have the real privilege of working with strivers, performers, and achievers every week, and I am noticing more burnout, more strain, and more pace every year. Reports show that workplace-specific stress and burnout are estimated to be an escalating issue across the country. UK wellness trends show that a staggering 65–75 per cent of workers in the UK have been affected by burnout in the last year (depending on measurement methods),[1] resulting in around 16 million people suffering, often silently, as more than 50 per cent of people are still not comfortable to talk openly about their mental health.[2] Around a third of workers were struggling with burnout just three months into 2025.[3] This kind of strain is not exclusive to work either. Reports show that the average Brit feels stressed for eight days a month – that's 96 days a year stressed out, with women, caregivers, and the unemployed at greater risk. These rates continue to increase year on year.[4] It's not going away, and we need to do something different to slow it down.

Do you feel it too? Have you noticed that ever-creeping sense of urgency and uncertainty that leaves you uneasy? Maybe things feel … less predictable than they used to. Does that map you hold in your mind about how to get from here to that notion you have of "success" feel a little vague right now, as we weave and bob through so much rapid change across many aspects of life? It can certainly feel overwhelming.

You're not alone. Many of us are questioning what we are doing and how we are living right now. Who is it working for to move so fast and take on so much? "Is it just me who can't keep up?" you might wonder quietly as you move along the continuum between just about coping and overwhelm, neither of which let you feel any real harmony in your life. Or perhaps you're asking yourself, "Why do I feel like I have less personal 'bandwidth' these days?" as your attention is being constantly extracted and you're doing your best to avoid the sense of impending doom coming at you from all angles. Maybe you are thinking, "Why don't I ever feel like I can put everything down and truly stop?" as you watch the rapidly shifting sands across cultural values, political landscapes, economic and climate uncertainty, and technological acceleration, all of which feel slippery and complex.

We have a mismatch – between our old notions of performance in life, and life as we actually find it today. Too often, that mismatch is leaving us teetering on the edge of exhaustion.

For me, burnout stemmed from the whirlwind of life choices I had made over the previous years, including the rush choice to move back to England from Australia where I had been for 20 years. My mum got sick, I panicked and felt way too far away, and so I jumped on the timely but underexplored opportunity of a job that would make it all possible. In a really brave move, my partner agreed to give up his job and come too. *Let's begin a new chapter – the farm, the retreat, the ducks, and the campervan; "We'll make it all work".* Elvis married us in Vegas, with our dog Paul as the best man, and I was on the 9pm flight to Manchester the same night. I started work two days later, straight into a football World Cup and on the road, while my partner was left dazed in a cottage in middle England, in the snow.

In true overperformer style, I needed to retrofit everything else in my life to make it OK to keep forcing and pushing forward. Pushing forward into the stimulation of big challenges is in part my nature, but in part my way of avoiding the pain of childhood wounds too. It was a very well-worn habit.

In between the practical weight of relocating and working out how things work in a new place with new paperwork and systems, a new job, and a new home, I resisted looking at the emotional weight of "being back" – back in a culture that was so familiar, yet I was so different. My initial nostalgia about being "home" gave way to readily triggered trauma, ghost-feelings I still held in my body from my young life, an earlier, wounded version of me battling for air time, but not sure if I wanted to be visible at all. I was always unsettled, a little vigilant. Un-spacious.

But I'm a psychologist and, in my role, I was a leader. My work required me to be spacious and be seen. I needed to do a lot of emotional labour, a lot of the kind of non-task leadership that absorbs time and emotional space and the kind of work that my mostly male counterparts often didn't notice. And so I gave everything to the work. My marriage was parched and in dire need of attention. I dipped in and out of my family of origin, always in role, rarely relaxed. Add Covid, another temporary European relocation, a second doctorate, a climbing accident with all sorts of dislocations and breaks, and I broke. I, like many of us, did not face the scale of change and pressure with the mindset of what I term a "regenerative performer".

Finding the Gears Again

My proposition in this book is that we haven't yet fully adapted our narratives and practices to a world that is exponentially changing, speeding up, and getting more demanding, and, as a result, we are "overperforming" too often and feeling the consequences of it. We are not built for this amount of more. In a world that is increasingly orientated to artificial intelligence, to machine-led and digital realms that make everything faster, it is essential that we reclaim and reorient ourselves to how real human beings work. Our ability to screech out a 110 per cent effort is designed to be an occasional gear that we use in moments of unusual pressure, and we can't live in this gear without losing all the rubber on the tyres.

Adapting to the elevated mental and emotional intensity of today requires something new. It isn't about simply coping with the way it is, gritting it out as you likely always do, and suffering through it for longer. And neither is it about getting to a point where you feel your only choice is to "down tools" or walk away from whatever area of your life you feel overstretched in, perhaps with a fantasy of a totally different life because this one isn't working anymore. A whole new life making artisan cheese in a coastal village may sound appealing, but it may not be the answer.

The thing is, many strivers and performers actually do (or did) like lots of aspects of their current lives … on paper. You may be building the life that you meant to, pursuing the professional life that you wanted to and creating the family and circle of friends that you dreamed of. Many of my clients still tell me they love lots of aspects of their life, but things just feel *too constant, too much*. Even the good stuff can make us feel this way if there is no give. If you're finding it hard to catch a breath or remember who you are and whether it's Tuesday or Thursday, it's not just you, as you will see in these pages.

Alternatively, you might be just getting started on building that life you imagined and feeling the crush. You might be questioning: "How do I get a foothold without feeling so … untethered?"; "Where does that foothold lead me if I do get one – into what kind of existence?"; "What do I want to participate in in this world, and do I have choices?"; "Do I have to do it like the Gen Xers who basically drank 'go-hard-or-go-home' Kool-Aid as their central food source? Or the Maximalists who never questioned whether more growth and more everything was right?"; "What if I want to consider my fellow humans and the planet in my choices – how can all that add up?"

This book is about cracking open those tired old mentalities so that you can emerge as a regenerative performer, *someone who knows how to access and create the kind of energy and approach that it takes to genuinely thrive, stay whole, and not feel like you are compromising what you care most about.* For you, that might be in your work, but it may also be about how you show up for other people, including those who come after your time in the world. If you're feeling dog-tired and stressed out, it might feel like a really big ask to start rethinking your approach to life. But check you out – you're here, considering it, with this book in your hands, and so you've already started to act in favour of yourself.

You don't have to change your whole life to feel good – or good again – but you may have to change your methods. My hope in *Life Reclaimed* is to help you with that, and I have a few decades of experience with some of the best performers in top-flight international sport, music, science, and business to draw on to support you.

About This Book

The arc of the book goes something like this. First, we'll talk about how we got here, to a place where all-encompassing seems to be our default operating mode and overwhelmed seems to increasingly describe our state of being as a result, and we name it, as overperformance.

I realise it seems crazy to think that we can overperform, or perform "too much". It's counterintuitive. We are born to perform. Every "how-to" lesson you ever had while growing up was in some way about learning to be a performer, and performing well may account for some of your proudest moments as a human being. Performing is necessary and desirable, and it *can be* massively rewarding – I know how good it feels to succeed, to finish, to complete, to master, to achieve. Part of why you feel great when you do perform is that you built up to it and you will come down from it, like a circle arcs up to the crest and then falls back down around the curve to create a whole shape. However, can you allow yourself *not to be performing* sometimes too? Or does that feel somehow … not OK?

Maybe a part of your performance lessons was about the kind of never-give-up relentlessness you ought to have, and the kind of aptitude for sucking up your emotions and getting stuff done that you ought to have too. Maybe you learned that the story you were in involved a race to the finish line and, if you stopped running, you'd fall and fail, and, worse, you would not have met your potential. Did you build your life values around these things?

The problem is that this isn't really a story that you chose for yourself, and being a character in that story can become exhausting, spiritually depleting, and, essentially, a bit disappointing. All of us live a life that grows out of stories. Culturally, we've built a whole bunch of performance ideas and motifs based on pushing ever harder. We have a set of narratives (stories told and retold by others about how things are until they are simply seen as "true") that act like reading glasses for the way we see things. Unless someone points out that those glasses are covered in smudges and can actually be taken off and cleaned up, it never crosses your mind that you could do something about the way you see life and the performance paths you're following!

As we explore in Part 1, these narratives are born out of industry. They are – and you probably have – an industrial mentality about performance.

Ex-athlete Selena's story offers an illustration:

> *My way of coping was to put in the hours and never stop to question. I thought I could force success into shape through time and tenacity, which is the way I dealt with most things; a habit I had learned as an athlete. Over time, I found myself absolutely exhausted and I started feeling like taking the time to recover physically and mentally was somehow "selfish". I was sleepwalking through my existence in order to get results, but, at the time, I just thought of it as not quitting. I had become a performance robot and I scared myself with the amount I was willing to give to results. The crazy part is how far away from my deepest cares and my dreams of being an ocean conservationist I got.*
>
> *One day, I got feedback from my team about sending emails at midnight and making urgent last-minute demands in a stressed-out tone that brought things to a head. I went home that day and thought, "My God, my own team are on the edge of putting in complaints about me because I'm asking them to work too hard." I was thinking about it the next morning driving in to work and I pulled out of a junction without looking and hit a cyclist. I thought I had killed him. When I went back home, in pieces, I finally had to admit to myself I was not OK and that I could only get through my work if I worked nights and weekends, lived*

> *with constant migraines and the sense of always being out of time. It took me to get to the brink before I could acknowledge my lack of self-care or care for others. I spoke to my boss and to HR and asked how I was supposed to get the actual job done. When they reviewed the work load, they responded by getting five new members of staff. I was terrifyingly slightly proud of that for a fleeting second.*

Do you recognise any of yourself in Selena? If not in behaviour, perhaps in the idea of pushing hard and closing yourself down to get the results being normal? If so, you have likely experienced overperformance.

Or perhaps Jake's story hits closer to home:

> *I've been working in the "fast fashion" industry for six years and increasingly unable to bridge the gap between what I am part of and what I know in my bones isn't OK. I have been hiding and pretending for years that I am OK – OK with the fast lifestyle, OK with the focus on squeezing every ounce of juice out of myself and out of the planet for the next must-have wardrobe "capsule" that no one really needs at all. I feel fake on so many levels, but I'm so far in and I can't clear my head to even think, and also no one forced me to do this. I feel stuck. Do I just … stick it out?*

What I hope to support with in these pages is to find the thread of your own industrial performance and overperformance mentalities and see whether they are really working for you – whether they are helping you to stand at your full height as a human being. You see, performance isn't all about outcomes; stuff you achieve "out there" in the world. You perform "who you are" too. You animate your identity with the choices you make and you live in to those identities every day. Every now and then, you might perform an identity so well that no one would realise, even you, that you have actually grown out of it, find it draining, and don't like it very much at all. You can end up depleted by who you are being, not just what you are doing.

When you are becoming ever more accomplished at performing versions of yourself that, in your quiet moments, you know *don't feel right or whole*, not only do you spend your life making impressions for other people in arenas and relationships that feel a bit artificial to you, but you smother all sorts of other, unexplored potential that is lying dormant in a dusty corner of your soul. Our job in this part of the book is to uproot those narratives so that later you might re-plant some practices and perspectives that actually nourish you and all the unique value you have to bring to the world.

Sometimes, you might overperform a part of your identity because you're not sure what else to do. Maybe you haven't had a supported opportunity to deeply consider who you are *now* in this place, in this world, and what it is that you want to perform at, before being enveloped in labels and diagnoses, roles, obligations, and the pull of status and opinions that drain away all of your glorious colour. Before your stories, mentalities, and personal history hooks you back into a game you might not even want to play.

In Part 2, we take a look at what happens when a person is smothering what they feel and starting to burn out. I am going to ask you to consider whether your overperformance might be a form of numbness that keeps the blinkers on and stops you lifting your head to look at what really needs your performance in the world, in your communities, in your home, and in your own life. Because when you stay numb, stressed out, overperforming, and busy, not only are you hurting, you are so much more likely to accidentally trample over things – life things, kinship things, relationship things – that actually matter deeply to your heart, but you simply have no more headspace for.

I have called this book *Life. Reclaimed.* Reclaiming is about recovering your natural state, which is not lazy and passive and unmotivated and in need of a good kick up the rear otherwise you'll never move at all, nor is it excessive, always-on, focused, fast, and flawless. This is about taking off those smudged glasses and starting to see more clearly. And, as you will see as we travel through these pages together, reclaiming agency in your own life will mean moving differently, travelling together, and making meaning.

Part 3 helps you to come home to yourself, gently, kindly, honestly, and bravely, so that you might start to live from what I call "wholebeing" – a way of living that does not require that you "just do you" and stay blinkered, or to ignore, shut down, dismiss, or compartmentalise whole parts of yourself so that the shiniest, most culturally conditioned parts of you can be out front, sprinting. We will explore the kind of values that support regenerative performance and see which of your values extract too much of your mental energy and might benefit from some evolution.

I think that now is a time for reclaiming what was always true for us – that we are already whole and we need to live and perform as whole people, not machines, not as perfect, straight arrows on target for greatness, and not in compartments and under the weight of our own enormous expectations.

It is so much easier to rise above the cut and thrust when you have done the work to see how you got into the scrap in the first place. This is your supported opportunity, these pages in your hands – a pause and a portal to recognise yourself anew.

Part 4 is about how you might take on life with the mindset and practices of a regenerative performer. In this section, I will share some of the practices I use with my clients in private sessions and in what I call "Slow Coaching", a deeper-dive form of coaching over a few days in wild, natural settings.

Regenerative performance involves moving from that industrial performance mentality to an ecological performance mentality. You will learn to move with life, not against it, and there is nothing more powerful for your performances than moving *with life*. You might find yourself asking, "Who and what do I need to start saying no to?" And you might start checking in with your gut, your breath, your nervous system, your environment, and your neighbour before you make your next move too.

The "muse" for this book – and much of my work – is nature-as-teacher, and the emphasis is on us getting beyond human-culture stories, which are man-made and temporary, to be able to also reconnect with human-nature stories; to connect with our ecological selves and look with fresh eyes at how we, and the rest of life, work – especially when it comes to ongoing performance.

You might be thinking that becoming a regenerative performer feels like a risk, a move away from what got you here. But it's a calculated risk based on clearer vision.

In nature, evolving always involves some risk. Take the magnificent transformation of the dragonfly for instance, one of the most ancient insects on earth, surviving for over 300 million years and predating even the dinosaurs. In the dead of night, the water nymph climbs out of the murky pond waters where it has lived as an aggressive underwater predator for the last three or more years; a grey, soft, shadowy, shedding, moulting creature. It climbs up a reed or grass stalk, into completely unfamiliar non-aquatic territory, in what seems like an insane move, triggered genetically, and it faces the sun. Over the coming days, it allows itself to dry out and crack open in order for a different, dormant but always present version of itself to emerge. The dragonfly's already-formed wings are forced open by the liquid spilling from its old body – wings that will allow it to fly in six directions: up, down, forwards, backwards, sideways, and to hover. The tightly bound thorax unfurls to release this iridescent creature. This transformation is paradigm shattering, creating a new reality.

Travelling through the ideas of this book is a bit like becoming that dragonfly. It requires you to trust your innate, natural centre – and that psychological change, mindset change, happens from the inside out. You don't need to wait for it to happen from the outside in as you battle to manage your scattered energy and weather the constant buffering of external events. You don't need someone else's blueprint or expertise. You need to slow down a minute to recognise yourself, the truth of your experiences, and your precious ability to sense once again what is right or not right for you, for "us".

The dragonfly eye is one of the most sophisticated eyes of any creature, made up of hexagonal fractals that allow it to see in multiple dimensions. That vision only comes after the struggle, the purposeful experience of cracking open and freeing up. It is difficult to allow some things to crack open on purpose in a culture that is about fixing and building and compounding our gains. This book is a simple invitation to trust yourself anew, and trust that regenerative performance can bring you a version of success that doesn't have to cost you your wholebeing.

PART 1.

HOW WE LEARNED
WHO TO BE

This section takes a look at how we become who we become, especially in relation to being performers. When I talk about you as a performer, I'm talking about all the ways you show up in your life, all the versions of you that engage with the world, and how you decided that those versions were good and right.

Some of how you learned who to be is simply science. It is about you being an innately complex entanglement of biology, neurology, electrical impulses, and chemistry. We are like giant ever-unfurling feedback loops bringing our unique human blueprints to life, repeating patterns, making new patterns; a physical design playing out in an infinite universe like a sparkler making a fleeting shape against the night sky.

We also learn "how to be" through the development of our psychology, which is, in turn, influenced by the culture and environments we grow in and the narratives that we have absorbed about how we ought to live. Our identities are formed this way, a back-and-forth conversation about who we can and should be or should not be, in which our narratives, myths, beliefs, values, and ways of seeing the world create another kind of feedback loop, this time directing our actions and understanding. It is here that we develop our sense of what is "normal" – how we are supposed to be if we want to fit in, and who dictates what normal even is.

In terms of performance, perhaps you learned that if you really enjoy and prioritise rest, you will get too comfortable, and complacency or laziness will quickly follow; or that those who perform best are better humans, most worthy of love and merit.

The continual signalling of these feedback loops shapes our experiences in profound ways, and taking a moment to stand back and consider them, and whether they are truly right, for you, for now, is where we start. It is incredible what can change for the better with a change of perspective and some fresh habits.

1.

STORIES THE WORLD TELLS US

Becoming you is a complex, magnificent process.

Anyone who has watched a child develop will attest to the wonder of witnessing a human being start to inhabit themselves. From an infant's very earliest moments of recognition of their own body and capability, learning to mimic and interact with caregivers, and using fine motor skills ("Hey, this hand can get this banana to my mouth!") to working out that they are a body that can move and explore independently, finding out "who am I" is an incredible thing.

A little later come the rivers of personality, the amusing quirks and hints of character that, by early childhood, might reverberate out in confident kid-wisdom and clear preferences (especially about how you, the adult, should be handling things!).

Watching a young child move freely, play as all mammals play, and role play as all human mammals role play, is watching them start to "become". Their thinking minds, fluid bodies, and vivid, precious imaginations are in a natural state, having not yet encountered the *quiet rules of the game* that will come to shape the way they see and live their lives.

Later, as children are socialised by parents, peers, institutions, and culture, they learn more sophisticated emotional survival skills.

They learn who they are supposed to be if they want to belong, be liked, feel safe, feel powerful, or get rewards and opportunities. This is a difficult dance that will be loaded with mistakes, failure, pain, struggles, and very big feelings for the child … even when it goes well. The dance of becoming is exquisitely sensitive to circumstance and inputs, and we all bear the markings of both in our adult lives.

And while much extraordinary work has been done on the psychology of development over the last couple of hundred years – work that has helped us understand ourselves and each other as human beings – that work has almost always operated on the assumption that a human being is an individual "vessel" whose job in life is to navigate through the world using a set of beliefs and understandings that are so normal to us that we can't even see them.

There is another way of understanding how we learned who to be, and that is through taking a look at how we were taught to see reality itself.

Some things we take as given, unquestioned, and obvious: like the "fact" that you are a separate individual in a separate body that belongs only to you; the "fact" that you are at the top of the food chain because humans are the smartest beings on earth and that entitles us to privileges; the "fact" that humans seek to be productive and need to reach their potential through careers and work, otherwise they lack meaning and will be dysfunctional; or the "fact" that our greatest asset is our mind and our bodies are basically like an Uber ride for those minds – a machine-like body to keep in good order, but not a centre of intelligence like the mind.

Each of these "facts" is what is called a narrative; a constantly retold set of stories, bits of evidence, beliefs, myths, symbols, and sequences of events that have been etched into our ways of being. Our narratives are so much part of the air that we breathe today that we no longer remember that, in fact, they are optional, changeable, and movable parts of our culture. And yet how often do we question the narratives we live by? About as often as a fish wonders what water is.

In her book, *The Myths We Live By*, Mary Midgley outlines how myths are everywhere in contemporary life, and those myths and narratives underpin the very fabric of who we think we are and what we think we should do.[5]

In political thought, they sit at the heart of theories of human nature – the story that there are always good guys and bad guys, and the stories about what kind of social contracts are good and right and should prevail (democracy?) and which are bad and wrong and should be quashed (totalitarianism?). Political narratives are full of stories about what kind of society people will accept without civil unrest (one with jobs, resources, safety, freedom, human rights?) and what kind they will not (one with slavery, cruelty, famine, corruption?). We don't have to look too far back or indeed too far across the globe to see that these narratives are not actually *true and inevitable.*

In economics, the myth of self-interest rules supreme – our Western narrative is that humans will always look out for themselves at the expense of others, especially when they are under pressure. Economic narratives also promote the belief that the "cream" (those with the most merit, those who are "most deserving") will rise to the top. And so an economic system like capitalism, where those at the top are seen to have earned it fairly, is therefore seen as not just pragmatic and just, but inevitable.

In the sciences still taught in classrooms, the idea of things being reducible to evidence and understandable/manageable only in parts remains a potent force. In human beings, those parts include bodies, minds, genders, and racial or ethnic groups, for example. Our scientific research is divided into expert disciplines, and our scientific institutions, practitioners, and modalities are usually specific and siloed, treating most aspects of life as categorisable. Midgley illuminates how deep and wide our need for scientific proof and "truth" has gone in modernity too – if we can't reduce a thing enough to explain or categorise it, we have historically been more likely to deny or denigrate it as irrelevant or fictional.

It doesn't matter that none of these political, economic, or scientific narratives are *true and inevitable*. It matters that they live rent-free in our psyches.

When it comes to our understanding of performance, our narratives also run deep – and, I believe, largely unchecked. And it is in these unexamined narratives that we have become pretty lost and strained as performers in an ever-faster, always-bigger, non-stop-better modern culture. It's these foundational beliefs and endlessly repeated stories that become the underbelly of our ways of being, our systems and structures and ideologies. And without us taking a fresh look at them, along with the recognition of those extraordinary internal feedback loops, which we'll explore in the next chapter, they can keep us locked into overperformance.

We imbibe narratives. They are written all over our interior landscape in invisible ink. They live in us and we live in them. It is through our narratives that we weave things into existence. Science shows us how atoms bond together to create capability in the body; in the same way our ideas, beliefs, and narratives bond together to create molecules of meaning.[6] Narratives provide stability and continuity in our lives. They help orient us, help us find purpose and identity. Narratives can help to ignite and nurture passion within us and they can also paralyse us with feelings of not being enough, of not being on-track. They are life-shaping, world-shaping, history-dictating, and future-making.

And the big news is, we have way more choice in which ones we live by than we might think. Choosing them is the first part of the process and practices that I will guide you through in this book.

So, what I'd like to do here is lift the lid a bit and take a peek in at four major narratives that I think are most associated with overperformance and see if there is anything you recognise.

They are:

1. The narrative of separateness
2. The narrative of exceptionalism
3. The narrative of optimisation
4. The narrative of more

Let's take a brief look at each.

1. The Narrative of Separateness

Do you believe that the course of your life is entirely up to you? That you are a traveller moving through the world and how it goes is largely a result of the choices that you make? When you think of the "you" that should be a success, are you thinking of you, the mind? And do you also find yourself, "the mind", issuing instructions to override your body or emotions when they signal that things are feeling a little … too much?

When you think of yourself as separate – independent from the rest of life – the weight upon your shoulders is tremendous. The responsibility of mentally dictating and controlling the outcome of your own existence and whether you "make it" by industrial, social, and economic measures, means that there is barely a gap in the incessant feeling that you haven't done enough or become enough; enough to be safe, to be finished, to belong, to be sure. We don't see ourselves as participants in the same nature as all other life; we see ourselves, at best, as stewards and, at worst, as overlords. We don't see ourselves as already whole, worthy, and complete; we see ourselves as unfinished, as not quite there yet – and we see the mind as the judge, the boss, and the pace-setter.

It starts with the deep and incorrect belief that we are separate from "nature", and our human experience of living is something entirely distinct, superior, and controllable. The rest of the living world might rattle and roll on by in its own rhythms, performing all its functions, but it's a backdrop for most people, most of the time. It's not much to do with us, right? Other than being a home and providing some natural resources for us to use (around 50 per cent of the resources that make up the world's GDP, in fact).

As the planet performs a few "small tasks" – like rotating on its axis to create night and day which allows you to see as light enters the retina and turns into an electrical signal to your brain; or fluctuating temperature and harmonising atmospheric pressure so that your blood can flow through your veins – you are busy being a separate human living in your mind, pushing yourself to rise above and achieve, and largely ignoring the rhythms and signalling of the earth that call you to sleep or wake, leap up and "make hay", or slow down and "winter".

As earth orbits around the sun to create seasons and make things for all beings to eat, while it creates the conditions that give rise to mycelium that can clean up man-made oil spills or is strong enough to build skyscrapers with, as it moves vast amounts of water between atmosphere, land, and water, creates both continents and cool breezes and handles the magnetic field that stops us from incinerating, us humans still harbour the view that we are largely independent, self-sufficient, and smarter.

This mental model of severance from earth and the rest of the living world is the underbelly of us thinking that we know best, that we can ignore and push beyond.

In his book, *Beyond Nature and Culture*, anthropologist Philippe Descola explores how we came to this story of separateness.[7] He explains how the West has artificially divided the world into culture and nature, what he terms as "the great separation". Descola explains that our narrative since the 15th century has always had man (gender specificity intended) at the centre of our imaginary construction of the way the world is, under a God-creator that favoured humankind above all else – everything else was "out there". We have a story of the *anthropos* – the human world in which our ideas about the self are giant – and it is surrounded by "the environment".

That "environment" became known as wild, and wild then became seen as unpredictable, exotic, random, uncontrollable, and also dangerous. Wild was the opposite of the supposedly civilised and intelligent realm of humans. And so nature and wilderness became seen as something to domesticate and tame, something less evolved than humans that needed controlling or "fencing off".

Not only has that narrative opened the door to our ideas about nature as inferior, a detached resource to endlessly extract from, rather than a life-sustaining system that we are a part of, it has spilled over into our ideas about "wildness" in ourselves. Today, we use terms like "running wild" to denote being distracted and "off-track". Running wild is seen as undesirable, rather than a natural state from which we have learned to conform and contort, and a wild person – perhaps a person who pays heed to the connection between the earth and their inner landscape – is seen as slightly odd; a spectacle.

Descola believes this "taming" was a wrong turn away from our deep human needs and the start of our angst as a species, who didn't recognise their speciousness anymore. We turned away from our own natures in order to avoid being out of synch with "civilised culture". And the defining feature of that culture for the last 200+ years has been industry, not ecology; productivity is king.

The idea that this one mammal, the human being, is separate from all other "nature" is kind of bizarre. There is brilliant science that illuminates how deeply entwined we are with the wild world. The extraordinary discoveries of scientist Lynn Margulis and her theory of symbiosis has fundamentally disproven that separateness is even possible between living beings, and that the idea of "individuals" is pretty fraught in biology overall – for example, by the time you are 70 years old, you will have 1,000 mites living just on your eyelashes and, right now, only about 43 per cent of you is genetically human.[8]

There is a mass of mini life forms within our bodily microbiomes, pressed up against each other, inside each other, consuming each other, and reproducing with each other, creating even more life forms. Life is entirely entangled, within us and around us. But our narratives have us seeing ourselves as separate selves inside a skin barrier, looking outwards at everything else.

We imagine ourselves to be different from "nature out there". Different enough to be able to override our physical needs until it is convenient – even the way we eat is based around breaks in work or educational performance. Different enough that we think we can ignore our own seasons and wedge life around our expectations – perhaps to be able to still do the work marathons and sprints that were available to you at 25 when you hit midlife, or to put off your fertility until it fits with your career in your early forties, or maybe to "push through" until your holidays on four to five hours' sleep after which you might pay attention to the fact that your head feels like it is on fire with stress and you have an incessant cold that hints at your withering immunity. It is a mentality of out-performing and overperforming that ignores who and what we are.

The narrative of separateness leads us to a place where we consider it progress when we can temporarily outsmart the natural ecosystems of both the human body and the earth body. As if we know more than the intelligence of life.

In his body of work on "ecological awakening", author and educator Bill Plotkin asks us to reflect on where the impetus to grow, build, make, or perform even comes from, noting that we have lost touch with the intuitive knowing that we are here to contribute to the whole web of life – we've forgotten our relationship with the world.[9] It is that web of life that compels us to "do", to grow, to make, to survive, and to thrive in the first place. We did all of these things before ideas of industry or personal performance took hold.

Yet, the further we drift from seeing ourselves as part of the planetary whole, the less we remember ourselves and the lonelier we get. We are mammals with predator and prey instincts (ones that show up in workplaces and teams and families and sports arenas and shopping malls). We read the vibrational energy rippling from another person, recognise movement patterns, and form a response to them way before a thought has kicked in or they have directly communicated with words or gestures. We are responsive to smells and temperatures, landscapes and light, and noise and types of food, something we repress when we expect the same unrelenting performance and routine from ourselves in the same conditions all year round.

Your body has extraordinary intelligence to share about what works best for living and performing. The world outside your window is full of wisdom too. You have the opportunity to perform in a way that does not reduce and deplete you until you are overperforming, exhausted, and a little lost – if you can start to recognise just how much you are part of life and not its master. Life, including planet earth, is a hardcore performer! But it works in a way that supports regeneration and sustainability. You can reconnect with that and move in the same way, as I hope you will continue to see through this book.

I recognise that it would be overwhelming and probably impossible to stay constantly attuned to just how interconnected we are (no one would get out of bed if we didn't at least feel we had a personhood with a skin barrier that wasn't being colonised by other life forms all day!). We've still got to get through the week, and most of us want to be focused and attuned to what we are doing. But could it be that our silent attachment to separation narratives does not allow us to *ever* notice our wholeness, our integrated lives, even when there is the kind of suffering that can lead us to crash and burn?

Modernity thinking is separation thinking: thought and emotion; body, mind, and soul; human and planet; man and woman; white and black. But in nature, the urge towards wholeness is ever-present. Transitions are part of wholeness: cycles, seasons, forging ahead, letting go, decay, renewal; everything is connected and everything harmonises to wholeness. Except us, wedded to the idea that we make the best blueprints for performing at life.

2. The Narrative of Exceptionalism

How we learned who to be also involves our narratives about the importance of being special or exceptional and, once again, it stems from ideas about who we are as humans in relation to all other forms of life. Exceptionalism came from the view that humans are not only qualitatively different from other animals and other parts of the living world, but that we are more important and greater in value. This splitting off also opened the door for the idea that, within the human race, some would be superior, more intelligent, and more deserving than others. The root narrative of "being better than others" has shown up forever in proclamations of superiority based on race, ethnicity, gender, sexuality, nationality, religion, profession, socio-economic status, and many forms of attainment. We decided that sameness, commonality, and ordinariness were not really OK.

Specialness is actually a radically inegalitarian idea. To be special is to be necessarily unique and unusual – uncommon – and it is what our culture strives for constantly. We look to be distinguished, and yet, at the same time as wanting to stand out, we desperately need to fit in. The only way to achieve that is to make it culturally normal and desirable to strive to be exceptional, to be extra-ordinary – to overperform.

In fact, ordinariness or being average are states that we think we need to get beyond, leave behind in our effortful "development". You might say out loud that to be a regular person, a member of the general public, or Joe Citizen is a noble and admirable thing, but the narrative sitting deeper and tugging at your psyche says you should probably be special if you want to be loved. You are supposed to be *accomplished*, right? As a professional, as a parent, as a partner, as a friend, as a relative, even in the way you show up in the world physically with exceptional looks for your age or an exceptionally good body.

Once that initial schism between the exceptional and the "mediocre" took root, a person could look around them and quickly work out that it was a smart idea to climb as high up as possible in all the pecking orders, all the categories of cool, because they are supposed to have as much social status as they can muster. That single narrative, that idea of being exceptional, drives our lives and our overperformance in unfathomable ways.

Take, for example, our cultural addiction to heroes and greatness. Heroes are seen as dynamic, seductive, more-than-just-human people – they wouldn't be heroes otherwise and we wouldn't be as wide-eyed about them. Heroes – public or personal – are seen as the expression of a superb spirit, and they are usually associated with courage, success, and integrity, doing things that only a select few could.

Hero worship and greatness are the cult of the individual and the cult of comparison. The hero is most often imagined standing alone, adored but not quite real. It is a strange, perhaps lonely, place to live for those who do breathe that rare air up there at the top – a life of appearances and tricks of confidence, public personas and sometimes feeling like the public image and the real person merge so much they can no longer be pulled apart without something breaking. And yet that status is coveted, and the pursuit of being seen as exceptional can take up a whole life and fill it with overperformance.

The whole you, the one who has been worn smooth like a river stone by mistakes and hardships and wrong turns, the one with flaws and chinks and quirks that radiate real life, starts to feel like the "more exceptional self" should be the identity that you wear in public, until you forget who you are under the mask. It is not random that the length and depth of our stories about needing to be exceptional coincide with overperformance and the level of overwhelm so many people are feeling.

In a 2024 podcast conversation with host Rich Roll, former US Surgeon General Vice Admiral Vivek Murthy expressed his deep concern about both kids and parents struggling under the weight of being exceptional and, importantly, needing to be witnessed being exceptional through the cult of social media.[10] He spoke about the increasingly overwhelming levels of extracurricular activities that parents feel are needed in order to give their child a good life, and to avoid them falling behind or not standing out. There is a lack of space for rest or play in a child's life as a result. In a *New York Times* op-ed piece, Dr Murthy said: "Parents struggle with loneliness at higher levels than people who don't have kids, feeling like they are constantly falling short when they look at social media."[11] Exceptionalism has a profound overperformance effect on the parent as much as the child, and because parents don't want to show their struggle and look like they are failing, they are suffering quietly and feeling increasingly isolated as a result.

Perhaps it is time for us to rethink exceptionalism and prioritise the idea that performing well actually looks like a human being of any age being able to feel whole and experience as much of life as possible. A child finding a sense of place and belonging, building deep relationships, learning who they are, and feeling integrated in the world is surely richer than always trying to rise above it. The most content people I have ever met allow themselves to experience the whole spectrum of human experience without feeling less if they are not at some artificial peak. They are also often absolutely viewed as a success. This isn't a choice you have to make between finding your best or feeling content; it's rethinking your *how*. This is how I hope to reframe performance for you.

3. The Narrative of Optimisation

When it comes to developing as performers, there are some narratives and myths that have really calcified in popular culture. They are mostly about productivity and optimisation; going ever-upwards as efficiently as you can and wasting no opportunities –

"you can sleep when you're dead". If you can optimise better than everyone else too, it is considered a bonus; you're on the fast track to the illusory finish line.

The myth is that, through endless effort and self-improvement, we can and should control all outcomes; it's up to us to max-out every possibility. If we can just squeeze every last ounce out of ourselves, we can make it.

The sentiment that gritty people do best and champions never quit is part of the story that we live by, and it is a notion that sits at the top of the slope towards perfectionism and depletion. We treat grit and go-get-it motivation as though we might have infinite reserves of the stuff, but, in truth, it is finite and needs regenerating and rebalancing. We treat perfect as the gold standard and, of course, "perfect" is a fleeting illusion.

The idea that endurance and relentless effort will drag us through to a better place – if we can just hold on – not only obscures the truth of performance, but it can leave us teetering on the dangerous edge of overperformance too. Most importantly, it can black-out our ability to consider alternative and important narratives we might live by, like curiosity, creativity, imagination, enjoyment, presence, reciprocity, and the power of strong relationships. As you travel through this process of reclaiming your life, we will explore how you can use each of these to better support and regenerate yourself.

The self-control and self-discipline required for an always-optimise mindset can often involve the suppression or rejection of emotion, especially when people have not yet learned to manage their range of emotions (like frustration, anger, and grief, for example) in a way that feels safe and socially acceptable. Squashing emotion is therefore particularly common in people who get stuck on the idea of needing to prove themselves through hard work. At times, this can lead to blind persistence, damaging stubbornness, and a big resistance to throwing in the towel and changing tack.

Busy and pushing becomes a badge of honour that demonstrates that we can't, or won't, slow or stop the conveyor belt, drop the ball, or be the weak link; "Not on my watch," we say. Machine-like, we keep on performing to the point of normalising depletion, resentment, and the anxiety sitting on our chests, as long as we are *productive*. This homogenous, un-diverse way of being denies a part of our humanity. *Homo sapien* or Homo ex-machina?

But the cultural echo chambers of pushing and overworking in workplaces are rife and we fear being the one to look slack and "request rest", to the point that even when we are struggling to find some space to breathe for a moment, it feels a bit like cheating or failing. An extremely high-performing, top-of-their-field client told me recently that they had a sense of under-working if they were not overworking.

If we believe that always optimising is the correct and best kind of growth and development we can have, we stay obsessively future-orientated. I believe that the kind of development that helps us to *seek life* is as much about working out how to enjoy and experience who you are and where you are today as it is about growing upwards through optimised efficiency. The narrative of optimisation has us buying into the idea that there isn't really any time to do things that don't add to productivity. That kind of thing is for "after" – after the finish line, after the end of the day, after all the tasks are done. We can think about all that when we "arrive" – except there is no arrival. This mentality never stops.

But, as you'll come to see, some of the "development" that supports performance might mean letting go, slowing down, opening up, going left and off-piste for a while, becoming wiser, maturing, responding to unexpected circumstance, or really honouring how we feel. It is about being able to shift and diversify, not drive through at all costs. But consider for a moment how hard it might be for you to contemplate changing in ways that didn't add to or improve you against external benchmarks. Continual climbing is a pretty hardwired narrative!

Optimisation narratives say we should constantly seek a control-based, outcome-based, brain-based, and productive life where we get stuff done and get good at as much stuff as we can, in order to feel successful. This is not necessarily a bad thing, but, like each of these four narratives that underpin overperformance, the drive to optimise can easily bleed into areas of life where it has no place, and where it becomes unhealthy and depleting – for example, one cannot "optimise" for the development of right, loving relationships with other people, or for the grace of maturing, for responding to tragedy with courage, or for healing a broken heart.

The term for feeling that it is necessary and desirable to improve and optimise, constantly, endlessly, for your whole life, is "schoolishness" (a term coined by social entrepreneur Akilah S. Richards)[12] – and it does not just stay in school. Schoolishness is about seeing everything as a graspable opportunity to be better and go further, rather than a learning opportunity for its own sake, or an activity that doesn't involve much learning or grading at all. Indeed, activities that are not about optimising might even feel wasteful to us. I argue that these non-outcome-based moments of simply feeling like you have nothing to prove are precious and rare, and an essential part of wanting to keep showing up and "doing life" in the first place. There is value in your experiences that don't end in efficient productivity too. We will dive into this a little more and develop some powerful tools for you to use in Chapter 8 when we look at better reasons to perform.

4. The Narrative of More

We live in a never-ending story about needing more. Whichever way you turn today, someone is going to be telling you that if only you could add this achievement or possession or upgrade, you would be a little closer to ideal, to complete and whole. Very often, that extra thing you absolutely need is something you can purchase. Just about every aspect of our existence has a relationship to the market: love, birth, death, food, mood, health, spirituality, sexuality, education.

There are two central ways that market-mindedness links to overperformance.

The first is that we are inclined to outsource our understanding of how we "should" be to experts and others who tell us what kind of "more" we need – what to do, who to be, and what to have in order to be seen to be successful. There is no aspect of our performance related to health, flourishing, appearance, well-being, intellect, entertainment, or structured play that does not have a long list of "ought to" consumables alongside it. I mean, are you really even on a run if you don't have a top-of-the-range wearable to tell you so? Or are you really ready for your summer break if you didn't buy a new wardrobe and get in shape with a six-week programme?

Take longevity, for example – how to have a longer life or health span. To sustain the days that you are still on the planet has, in some cases, become a zone of competition and performance. Life itself has become something curatable through chasing more, optimising for the future, and, most importantly, consuming correctly. For me, this is anything but health. It is passive outsourcing of our worth to the market and all of its brands, whose very existence is dependent on you never feeling like you have consumed enough.

I smiled wryly at an ironic Instagram post by @ryanlloydhaynes that went like this:

> *Hiya. I just wanted to confirm that everyone else was doing like, no screen time before bed, sleeping in a cold room with no coffee before 11am, warm water with lemon as soon as you open your eyes but no phone for the first two hours, sunlight in your third eye first thing, red light therapy for half an hour, 10,000 steps a day, an ultramarathon with no social media, 12 eggs, raw goat's milk with three avocados, two raw steaks and a full plant-based diet dipped down in magnesium spray with ashwagandha, zinc, vitamin B12, sauna, gym,*

cold therapy, but only before the gym because that affects the gains, electrolytes, hit your protein goals, two litres of water, but please God, not tap water, no gellan gum, sucralose, sugar, sweeteners, no porn, meditation for half an hour a day, all whilst completing a Hyrox and microdosing whilst replying to 34 WhatsApps, 6 of which are 3-minute long voice notes, checking in with your friends and family, maintaining a relationship, writing in your gratitude journal whilst going to therapy, and not to mention a job and kids. Just checking everyone else is doing that?[13]

The second big issue with the narrative of more is that it leaves us in a position where we can start to perceive that our lives only have real value in so far as we have the ability to keep gaining – more stuff, more trappings of success, more status, more money.

For me, this "more culture" disconnects us from soul, from each other, and from the living world, because it leaves us valuing consuming and gaining so highly that we will choose not to look up and see the cost we wreak in this opaque mission for more.

Perhaps we need to give value to that which is not "more stuff", and that which exists apart from money. Things like sharing, reciprocating, relating, making. Things like beauty, care, movement, love, community. These are free and organic, and even though attempts are made at commodifying each of these things, can we recognise that they are precious, important, and already real, outside of the narrative of more? You don't need to earn money or spend money to have them; they are already valid and important if they call you. As a regenerative performer, you will rest easy in the knowledge that the choices you make about how you live are choices made with your heart and your wholebeing as central. You will see that you don't need a "be-more-have-more-do-more" measuring stick to recognise your worth.

And so perhaps you, like many of the people I have worked with, find yourself with a set of understandings, beliefs, ideas, and especially cultural stories about "how we ought to be" that have become so embedded that they trump the evidence right in front of you, especially the evidence about how you are feeling if you are kind of stretched, kind of unfulfilled, kind of anxious that the finish line doesn't seem to be coming into view. Again, this is not just you. We will ignore how we feel in favour of the cultural narratives time and time again, because they are so extraordinarily normalised. We drink in this tech-based, industrial, individualistic, information-based, and rapidly globalising culture every day – it is how we have learned who to be and it is coded into our nervous system at some level, and so even when we know – "Hey, some of this just doesn't feel right" – it's still quite hard to face it. To not live by these narratives might even feel … a bit like failing, which is why I am strongly encouraging you to think about becoming a regenerative performer from two fronts. First, finding and shaking out your performance narratives and, only then, developing some better practices to work with. If you don't change the way you see, the methods will be easy to forget in a month or two.

That feels big, right? Shaking out lifelong narratives? You can start by catching the small stuff first. As your performance stories have accumulated unchecked, they may have, in places, become toxic and seem just too big to move. Nature might offer us an example of the power of starting small.

The Build-Up of Our Overperformance Ideas

In biology, the term "bioaccumulation" refers to the process where pollutants or toxins build up within an organism so much that the organism itself starts to become toxic or poisoned. The "little bit" of toxin on its own doesn't seem so drastic, but when all those "little bits" add up, the organism can't cope or becomes poisoned.

Take a fish, for example, swimming around in polluted seas full of plastic, pesticides, heavy metals like mercury, and synthetic hormones from human industrial activity. The fish takes in these substances, but they are not easy for the fish to metabolise or get rid of, because these substances are not natural and organic and the fish has not evolved to handle these kinds of inputs and conditions, so they become part of the fish. When the fish is taking in more toxins than it can get rid of, it will itself become toxic to the next thing that comes along and eats it.

So, the toxins taken in by little fish become part of that fish. The next middle-sized fish that comes along has been swimming around in the pollutants too and has toxins in its body that it can't get rid of, and then it eats the small fish too and doubles the trouble. Toxins pass up the food chain in this way, and each predator is not only swimming in toxic seas themselves, they are consuming toxic food. Eventually, the biggest fish are the most toxic (tuna, anyone?), even though every part of the life cycle and food chain is affected.

It's kind of the same with our ideas and narratives: there is a "food chain" of stories and myths that we don't deliberately choose to consume, but they are so much part of our environment and cultural diet that we don't even notice them. The "big fish" are like our institutions and social settings, and the small fish are like me and you; individuals who cannot necessarily change the seas we swim in directly, but we can change our own diet of ideas, beliefs, and narratives quite deliberately, an act that fundamentally creates ripples for others too.

If our overperformance narratives were already obvious and clear and we could see that they were directly causing us harm, of course, most of the time we'd avoid them. Something small and maybe slightly toxic on its own – let's say, a particularly extractive workplace that wants more from you than it is healthy for you to give – might feel like an independent, one-off overperformance driver that you can avoid: "I'm not taking in that poison, thanks!" Great move; an act of reclaiming your life. But our cultural stories are a patchwork of slightly blurry things that build up, rather than a single, solid thing on its own. They are the sea, not just the fish, and so we don't always notice what drives us to overperform.

We are all swimming in that narrative sea all of the time – narratives that say that you are separate and can remain unaffected, that your purpose is to be better, that you can get to wholeness and success by optimising and working harder, and that having more of everything will solve all the problems. These stories have accumulated both within us and around us. They affect all of us.

We rarely take a step back to decide how we are going to see the world, we are just … in it, seeing and being. Maybe it never even occurred to you that you can change the way you see; that all of your performances in life could be done without the heavy weight of negative narratives, or that you could decide that regenerating your energy and feeling whole were the point.

When we do start to see cracks in our own world view, noticing things don't quite add up as we view the world through our little lens, and maybe as we stop numbing out quite so much, we reach a point where we have a choice; the continual "bioaccumulation" of toxic old ideas isn't the only option. You can feed yourself on a different diet of narratives; you don't have to be stuck with the "same old" mush.

Imagine detoxing some of your industrial mentalities – those stories in your head that say only the "biggest fish" can make change and you are not big enough or powerful enough to exert such an influence.

Imagine realising that the industrial mentality that insistently tells you that your own worth and greatness are just around the corner if only you can keep on giving 110 per cent and don't miss your window of opportunity is *just one story*.

What if you knew that change can come from any direction and can come out of seeming chaos – even those moments when we feel broken and totally out of gas?

What if you knew that life is way less predictable, more mysterious, and more awe-inspiring than you think?

What if you reimagined the idea of losing out and not reaching your potential, and, instead, you started to see your potential as more to do with the level of aliveness and presence that you feel in your one precious life?

Life is so full of vitality and alive, but holding on to what has finished is futile. Those old ideas and narratives need to go in the "psychological compost bin" where they can rot down and be transformed into something more fertile, something in a new form. Then you might start to recognise the new life in your ideas and stories about how it is, how you are – the small sprigs of new vitality that grow out of your courage to let the old rot away. That is the goal of *Life. Reclaimed.*

When you compost waste in the garden, it can start to stink if you don't turn it over now and then. The waste material needs air to break down properly and to avoid getting too hot. In fact, if your compost pile is left exposed to the heat with no attention paid, it can literally set on fire. It's the same with composting our psychological "waste". Too much exposure all at once and then ignoring it or avoiding it makes change feel too hot and high-risk. But if you let things break down well by turning them over, giving them airtime, adding some self-compassion, some things to promote balance, and some support here and there, and you allow sufficient time for the process, you can end up with very good psychological soil to grow your new narratives and ideas in.

Paying attention to your deep stories and narratives about your performances in life is the first, brave step to freeing yourself from chronic overperformance and becoming a regenerative performer. What can you fish out from the four cultural narratives we have explored here? Perhaps a flicker of recognition about your own sense of separateness or need to be superior and exceptional. Perhaps a glimpse of your own patterns of never-ending optimisation and seeking more. It's great if you can see it, even if it makes you cringe. You've started. You have so much to look forward to as a regenerative performer.

2.

STORIES YOU TELL YOURSELF

If all of us are swimming around in cultural narratives that the world feeds to us, surely at some point we'd recognise them and think, hey you know what, that story of endlessly needing more, or needing to be exceptional, or being different to the rest of life and the rules of rest, renewal, or change not applying – I don't really believe in those things. They don't make sense when I really think about it, not for me or not for this moment in time, and so I'm just going to stop letting them provide my road map for life. Right? Can we just get off the bus at this stop, please?

Recognising your cultural narratives is a brilliant, crucial start, but there is more of your performance picture to develop. Starting to see the stories the world tells you about how to perform at being "you" is like putting a frame around a photograph. Bringing the photograph into focus will require you to uncover and recognise the stories that you tell yourself about performance too; your personal, internal beliefs and mentalities that are shaped from your life experiences – things you enjoyed and avoided, things you got rewarded for or were taught to resist, attitudes that your family and your environment shaped and continue to shape, and, importantly, your physical and emotional state. This last part, especially, can be very much linked to trauma, and we will dive into that in depth in the next chapter so that you can bring your full performance picture into sharp focus. It's from there you can ask:

- What do I care enough about that it drives me to perform well in life?
- What triggers me to overperform and get to that place where I can't "put it all down" for a moment?
- Where do I close parts of myself down so that I can keep overperforming, even to my detriment?
- How big is the gap between the stories I live in (outside narratives and inside mentalities) and what I feel like I need, and want, in my heart?

In this chapter, we're going to look at some common personal overperformance mentalities, before taking a look at the kind of feedback loops that keep you hooked in.

But first, let me introduce you to Merlin:

Reflecting back, I can see how my need to overperform took root.

I was born to a couple in conflict. My dad left within a year of me being born. And that's probably the foundation of my sense of self. Not good enough. Literally born to fail.

As I child, I didn't know any of this, of course. I was quiet. Well behaved. Smart. I worked hard, and got good grades. I was the responsible one. Everything my mum could ask for. I centred my self around the "good son" label. I loved her. And I knew she needed me. I knew how fragile she was.

Medical school was a sure thing. And there my ascension continued. Merits. Distinctions. Awards. And on graduation, admission to the top training programme in my chosen central London teaching hospital. Things kept falling into place. I found myself on a fast-track in surgery. Identified as one to watch. Success assured. Path set.

And here's where the wheels started to get a little wobbly. I'd never really questioned the nature of my reality. My life. What it was for. What I actually wanted to do. My entire life so far had been on autopilot. I worked hard because that's what was expected. I did well because that was expected. There was no other way. My self-worth was totally tied to achievement, and achievement was determined by the measures of others.

Don't get me wrong. I enjoyed medicine. I loved surgery. I enjoyed the challenge of it. And the ability to help people. To be respected by others. But I also had a nagging feeling that I didn't deserve any of it. I had fallen into this life and, at any moment, people would realise what a fraud I was. As I became more senior, I started to become more afraid that I wouldn't be as good as people expected.

I had also started to become disillusioned. I felt like a cog in a machine. Doing the same thing day after day. And for what? Who was I really? Did I even matter? I knew I could pretend to be "successful". But why did the thought of that leave me so empty?

My drive to override these feelings probably did lead me to double-down and "overperform" until I was close to snapping physically and mentally, and I had no idea what to do with how I felt. I was anxious and numb.

And then the next chapter. A chat and invitation over a drink after work. Welcome to the world of start-ups. The world of tech. I was filled with purpose again. Things that I did meant something again. I could create.

But dealing with the shame of leaving medicine was hard. Nobody could believe it. People literally called me crazy to my face. They told me that I was bound to fail. Medicine was my identity. Shedding it was one of the hardest things that I've done.

For the first few years, start-up life was great. I felt purposeful, like I was going to make a difference to the world. I wanted to perform, to feel the challenge in it. Then things started to change.

My days shifted from creating to continual fundraising. The move towards more personal authenticity slowly slid into a "fake it till you make it" mentality, an "I'm smashing it" mask. My echo chamber was filled with people believing we were amazing, while I could see all the problems, all the profits over people, and the always-on/never-off culture. But I had to maintain that mask, that performance.

Eventually we got acquired as a business by a large pharmaceutical company. But the need to perform just continued. Profits over people worsened. I was working against my values. I wasn't being true. And the performance was making me ill.

I spiralled. Lost all shape and function. Became goo. Useless. Used up. Full of shame. Even though on the outside all anyone would see was success.

When I heard this story for the first time, I felt it down to the bone.

For his whole life, Merlin expanded like injectable foam into every corner and crevice of the contemporary "what it takes to win" mould. He had an abundance of genuine talent, he had choices and resources, he applied himself willingly, and, by most objective measures of performance, he really was smashing it. He loved performing. Most people love performing! So, why did it spill over into pain?

In part, because while Merlin had mastered (and relished) the hustle, he stopped being able to connect with his own feelings that were whispering, "Hey, this success is only on paper. It is material success, but not emotional or spiritual success. It feels very different than I thought it would. It's not where my heart is, or my values, or my creativity. And it's making me sad, and confused." The thought that accompanied these feelings was, "It doesn't make sense to feel this; there must be something wrong with me."

I believe that Merlin also likely felt like an imposter, against all evidence to the contrary, because he really was living someone else's life, being a star in someone else's sky, not his own.

These feelings probably felt messy and irrational to Merlin, to the extent that he repressed and buried them and pretended everything was great to most people around him. He put on a performance mask – a version of himself that seemed to make more sense in terms of the cultural narratives he grew up with and the personal performance mentalities he held quietly inside – and he hid his true feelings behind that mask, until he started to feel unwell.

What started as genuine passion turned into a constant act; a painful pretence on the outside while feeling something completely different in his inner world. His personal performance mentalities had him believing that to change, or to stop now, would be akin to failing. He'd come too far and ticked too many boxes already, and he could not work out how to face that – hiding and masking and driving himself to keep going felt easier.

Merlin's childhood was relevant too. Trauma in his case came in the form of feeling that he had to play a role (the perfect, dependable son who could fill the void in his mother's emotional life) in order to be fully loved and safe. When it comes to the sense-making that children do about such matters, truth and fact and parental intention matter much less than what is felt. Merlin loved his mum so much that he wanted to be perfect and please her, and he needed to feel that his place in her universe was assured too. In his mind, working very hard and being brilliant was the thing that pleased her most – and so he adopted an internal, unspoken "no-fail" policy. When he started to realise that his choices were unfulfilling and deadening, his heart broke under the weight of that child-made idea that he would be a terrible disappointment. And so he drove himself into the ground pretending, all the while drifting further from his own true north. He told himself he could compartmentalise his feelings, and they didn't matter much anyway. I see many "Merlins" – talented people who drive themselves into the ground in some way because it seems easier than facing their truths, until that is, they can come home to themselves and reclaim a little more of who they really are, from the inside-out, through the kind of work you and I are starting in this book.

Let's take a closer look at some of the stories we tell ourselves about who and how we should be in relation to performance; mentalities that, like Merlin, can leave us at the top of a slippery slope to pretending and pain.

The "Straight and Neat" Mentality

When we think about a successful life, we often imagine it as a series of successes that build upon one another. From our earliest achievements, we hear comments such as, "Next you will be ready for/able to…" Even after falling in love, you may well have heard, "So, when are you going to move in together/get engaged?" and then, "When do you think you might have kids?" – as if the plan is set and known universally, and it would be odd to dissent from it. Likewise, in work, when success comes, everyone's eyes immediately look to the horizon once again to see what is next in order for you to achieve your potential. Going "off-piste" to experience something else is reserved for the young and the retired, and can be seen as radical or reckless for someone deep in the belly of their career and their financial commitments.

It starts to feel logical to travel only in straight lines (they let you go faster) and to make only "sensible" decisions that support your productivity and your future ambitions to be better, go further, and have more; the industrial lens on life that we explored in the last chapter. The mentality that builds up around this is that you have no time right now to listen to your feelings or your wandering thoughts about what and who else you might be, or even about not feeling so great – you'll think about that later, when you have a break. Right now, the best thing to do is to keep your eyes on the road and keep driving. It is a performance mentality that serves you in achieving predetermined outcomes, but does nothing for your ability to lift your head up and respond to the life you find yourself in.

The "Sunk Costs" Mentality

Another part of our mass participation in chronic overperformance, even when it is destructive to us, is the notion of sunk costs: "So much has already been invested, I can't stop now." These sunk costs might include time, energy, and money, but they also cover reputation, risks we took, things we denied ourselves, choices we died on the hill for, and, most importantly, emotional investments – especially in relationships. I have listened to countless stories of couples who are ill-matched or have outgrown their common connections, but they push through "for the kids" or because "it used to be so great". Or, like Merlin, people who felt that so much had already been invested into a professional path and so much expectation was hanging off that sunk cost, that they push on into unhappiness.

Sometimes, we hang on to the gains and the credits and the image other people have of us, long after they have stopped working for us. The unspoken "sacrifice ledger" that we have in our minds is a powerful force: "I have given so much, I should at least wait around for the return on my investment in the future." The ledger is underpinned in part by ideas about what you deserve, especially when you have struggled. What returns would make all of your sacrifices worth it for you? Your social status? How your kids turn out? Where your career takes you? What kind of health you will enjoy for all of your efforts in the gym and for the truly enormous sacrifice of drinking apple cider vinegar? What kind of love you deserve in future relationships? How much cash you made?

The performance mentality that builds up around sunk costs is that there has been too high a price paid, too much sacrifice made for it not to count – you can't waste the effort.

From a nature perspective, there can be no waste. If something no longer serves its purpose in the natural world, it is time for it to either die off and feed the cycle of life, or adapt to the circumstances and environment and find a new niche. There is no judgement about changing direction in nature; change is a necessary principle of thriving. If it doesn't work anymore, there is no need to hoard it. Sunk costs are not always buried treasure.

The "Once I Cross the Line" Mentality

A particularly powerful performance mentality that I have encountered over and again in elite sport is the idea that things will change, and a person will change, after this unmissable window of opportunity has passed, once this intense period is over. After that, you'll start caring for yourself a little better. When you cross the finish line, you'll be able to be a little bit less self-focused and closed off, a little more available for your relationships. After that, your stress cycle will be less intense and you will be way better at handling your mood swings and yes, sure, you'll go get that mammogram or check out those headaches, you'll squeeze in that lunch with your best friend.

The thing is, that hectic period never really ends, does it? Not by choice or not for long anyway. We get addicted to pace and pressure – quite literally. That fast-paced thrill comes with a regular bolt of adrenalin. Being rewarded and celebrated for your superhuman efforts comes with a hit of oxytocin. Even physically rushing and pushing can release endorphins and a cascade of other chemicals that make being on the edge feel totally normal.

Operating under strain creates a neural feedback loop that makes strain and success seem automatically linked, to the point where you may even find yourself a little restless and uneasy if you are not straining. These changes can not only become neurologically hardwired over time, they can become a bad psychological habit too – one where you find yourself defending your right to overperform and be in your own "hurt locker", your own "air lock" of effort, regardless of the cost to yourself or to those around you. You might name it as commitment, but it also looks a lot like being constantly uncomfortable with where you are now, and it may leave you feeling pretty lonely if the finish line does ever come.

The "One Shot at My Potential" Mentality

I recall a semi-pro athlete who had been told that she had the potential to be an Olympian in her sport. She worked her heart out, every spare minute of the weekends, long drives to be able to train in the right conditions, freezing cold early-morning rides in the pitch black, the competitions, the right preparation and recovery, saying no to career roles that didn't offer her enough flexibility because she didn't want to waste this opportunity, waste her talent and potential. She was winning, performing, becoming a champion.

But she hated it. Not the kind of loathing that comes with having to get out of bed and make your body hurt from effort, and then, 30 minutes later, in motion, you relish the challenge, the fact that you are capable of it and the surge of purpose. Instead it is the kind of dislike that comes from a lack of passion, an absence of love. Many athletes hate the training, but it's love–hate. In this case, there was just no soul in it for her.

The humming anxiety in her chest was from performing without desire and alignment – overperforming – and it was ever-present. The block in her throat that didn't allow her to speak her truth was the idea of waste; wasted talent, wasted effort, wasted time. What would people think? How could she live with the fact that she turned away from her potential? Everyone knows that these opportunities don't come around again. How could she miss her "one shot"?

She was heading for a fall, too focused on her labels and the role she played in other people's imaginations – her family, her coaches, her followers, her competitors – rather than on what she herself was capable of and called to. Eventually, she unearthed the courage to be honest, say it out loud, and stop the chase. The relief was palpable and, for her, facing the fact that she did not want to pursue that sport at that level was a sort of call to unleash who she really was; the person behind the shirt.

The mentality that we have one shot at becoming our full and whole selves leads us down the path to overperformance and pain. The alternative mentality is that something like your potential will quite literally take your whole life to understand, and cannot possibly be reduced into a single result or achievement. Your worth to the world cannot be understood in such small ways.

In truth, you don't have to be one thing, but you also don't have to be all things either. You don't have to know your one true calling or your purpose in order to prove your worth to anyone. Maybe you have multiple purposes and potentials. Author Emma Gannon uses the term "multi-hyphenates" to describe people who put their energy into several different endeavours at once.[14] Other terms include multi-pods, polymaths, renaissance people; people who express their life force in various ways or for whom experience and expression might be more important than elevation. We're not used to thinking about potential as width and diversity as well as height and mastery. But I think a concept as huge as "your potential" requires us to think about the whole of you.

When I coach high performers one-on-one, I always introduce my approach as both helping people succeed at "their thing" while staying in one piece as a human being and, importantly, being here for the experience. Isn't that the joy of achieving anyway?

The "Need to Control How I Am Seen" Mentality

Most of us care about how we are seen, at least to some degree. Sometimes, that care can look a little more like control. "Impression management" or "self-presentation" can be described as a conscious or subconscious process in which people attempt to influence and guide the perceptions of other people in social situations by presenting themselves in favourable ways that satisfy their own needs and goals. These needs and goals might be to be liked, ingratiated, favoured, to be seen as successful or competent, to be respected, accepted, held in high regard, or seen as attractive, for example.

We prefer to present the best side of ourselves and make a good impression, naturally. But for some people, a kind of vigilance develops where you want to present *only* the best version of yourself to the world – even to your loved ones – and it can really keep you hooked into overperformance and pretending.

Do you find yourself separating out the occasionally boring, less attractive, slightly self-absorbed, or unentertaining aspects of yourself and putting a filter of some kind over them? Do you think twice about the image you are presenting and whether it is up to scratch to the watching world? It's a 24/7 performance vigil and it's really tiring. The weightiest stressors in human beings are emotional ones. The biggest stressor of all is pretending to be who you are not.

It seems rational to be vigilant about the face you show to the world when you feel that you are being watched and critiqued incessantly – and, increasingly, it does feel that our lives are being lived unveiled and in full public view. But it has costs, and those costs include being addicted to looking successful, and behaving or presenting yourself in ways that might please other people, but that steal your presence and create anxiety. The mentality here is that you won't be enough if you show yourself as you naturally are, and so you'd better be on your game full time, embellishing and upgrading as you go. It is in part a response to threat; the threat that you will be evaluated badly and rejected by society.

Sally Dickerson and her colleagues at UC Irvine found that social evaluative threat (SET) is more powerful than the threat of financial insecurity, health worries, work strains and pressures, or too many demands on our time.[15] Social evaluation brings the risk of shame, possibly the most powerful emotion of all, which relates almost exclusively to the judgement of others. Feeling rejected and shamed is a strong immunity dampener and can literally make us feel unwell, reaching where even sadness, anxiety, general stress, and depression don't.

Social media and online life are full of social evaluation – in fact, that is their primary mechanism for keeping your attention. They are designed to make you care about how you are seen. But being caught up in presenting yourself and managing the impression you make isn't just about the time you spend on or preparing to be on social media, it's about the trail of perfection that begins to follow you around once you step back into real life and feel like you don't measure up – the "likes" are always at risk.

I had a younger client who lives in the public eye, who, for 18 months, rose 90 minutes earlier than her more-famous partner just to ensure that he would never see her without make-up or "being ready", and so that the first social media posts of the day were curated and "brand-optimal" for them as a couple. She lived with low-level performance anxiety at every moment, never exhaling into her more honest, most appealing self until the emotional fatigue of the pretence caught up with her and she started to crack. The crack was wholly welcomed by her partner, as it turned out. He desperately wanted to be normal and unfiltered when he had the chance, at home.

The threat of negative social evaluation can hijack our neural reward system significantly. It's what Jonathan Haidt described as "a pocket full of poison" in his book *The Anxious Generation*.[16] And where social media algorithms are concerned, very often the hijack is done with the intention of keeping us tied to performing and consuming. Being witnessed constantly, even in your own home and from the device in your own hand which you are holding to your own face, profoundly amplifies our penchant for instant gratification. It keeps you hooked on you, and less able to connect to here, to others, to real life.

Each of these personal performance mentalities starts out in your mind with the intention of helping you to succeed, but is caught in culture. Culture that emphasises control, force, and top-down influence instead of organic renewal and resurgence. Culture that pays only lip service to collective flourishing or mutual support and creates systems that force individual, independent striving and "first-past-the-post" lifestyles. These mentalities deny wholeness – your own wholeness as a person and the wholeness of our society. Overperformance isn't random; it is a result of the rules of the game. And it isn't your fault. But there is a lot you can do to step out of the circus and come home to yourself, once you can see.

Living your life in mentalities that encourage you to ignore yourself and push on teaches you to close off your feelings. You learn to become hyper-focused and singular, and to create a shield with the notion that this is what excellence requires. You get used to rationalising, denying, and justifying to yourself why it is important for you to act this way. It's a form of self-gaslighting; denying what is real for you in favour of what lets you feel some control or safety.

Gaslighting Yourself

If I were sitting with you right now, I would want to ask you how you gaslight yourself the most in relation to overperforming:

- Do you regularly ignore your needs, the craving for diverse activity or interests, so that you can keep being industrious and "get ahead"?

- Do you shame and blame yourself a little if you do less than you thought you could?
- Do you criticise yourself for not being as far ahead or as good as you want?
- Do you feel guilty when you pause, slow down, or rest?

Gaslighting is described as a harmful psychological manipulation that causes a person to doubt their own experiences. When being gaslit, a person might question their own perception of reality, their memories and recollections, and their own judgement, and it is usually employed by someone willing to abuse another person for their own gain, control, or comfort. A simple example is when a person forgets something important that you told them, and then denies that you ever told them in the first place. Or perhaps you let someone know that a comment they made hurt you, and they deny making the comment or tell you that you are too dramatic and it was just a joke. The feeling you are left with is confusion and uneasiness.

When we self-gaslight, similarly, we deny, diminish, or belittle our own experiences to the point where we no longer trust ourselves fully. Merlin did this in the earlier case study when he started to feel like a fraud who was about to get found out, rather than facing the fact he wasn't loving what his performance mentality told him he should be loving. Instead of aligning our thoughts, feelings, perceptions, and experiences openly, we cover over the gap between them and a barrage of internal self-criticism is unleashed to keep us away from that gap. It's like neglecting or bullying yourself. It might look like second-guessing your memory of what actually happened (when someone at work brought your deadline forward by two weeks and you had holiday booked), telling yourself that it was your own pathetic poor planning and dreadful communication that was the problem, and ignoring how you really felt about it (angry, frustrated, anxious, fatigued).

"Why would we do that?" you may ask. Because squaring up to the real recollections and feelings either doesn't quite feel safe or feels too consequential – too far away from how you think you *should* feel and how you think you need to act in order to stay on track. It may be more accessible for some of you to think that your feelings are irrational and unreasonable than to acknowledge that someone or something has really pissed you off, hurt you, or is causing you distress. You dismiss yourself as not a clear thinker or reliable witness to your own life. If you carry one or several of the overperformance mentalities we discussed above, you will do what you can to close the gap between what your mentality dictates you should feel, think, and experience, and what your experience really is – even at the cost of your self-compassion.

Self-gaslighting is devastating. When you regularly ignore the gnawing ache in your stomach or the shaky hands, the flush of dizziness and the hot tears standing in the checkout queue at the supermarket, and when you simultaneously admonish yourself for being too weak or too soft, you are gaslighting yourself. When the kids ask you to drop them off at their friend's for a PlayStation session and it's the fifth time you have got in the car that weekend to meet their social agenda and you are exhausted and overwhelmed, you say no, and then call yourself a terrible parent, you are gaslighting yourself.

Self-gaslighting is especially prevalent for anyone who has bought into the idea that they specifically, or "people like them", need to meet higher benchmarks than everyone else because they have more to prove and less room to move. Brilliant autistic and dyslexic leaders I have worked with push themselves and mask their realities more than others in one-size-fits-all back-to-back meeting cultures with heavy requirements to plough through written documentation beforehand. Black and brown leaders who are not equally represented might feel the need to out-perform everyone else in order to be seen, and be seen well – reinforcing the normality of expecting to have, to be, and to do more than others, and thus operating from depletion.

If you can catch yourself before you gaslight and before the entrenched performance mentalities kick in, you might get to see what your overperformance template really says. Does it say that all this might be valid, but the most important thing is still to get the (industrial) results, and be seen to be getting the results, whatever the costs to yourself? Does it say that you don't have an option, because it is the way it's done and everyone does it? Does it say that you have to keep proving – to yourself and to others – that you can do whatever it takes? A friend of mine passed out on a flight after ignoring his debilitating symptoms of light-headedness, nausea, headaches, blurry vision, and unusual levels of fatigue for months on end, and telling himself that he just needed a nap, could rest on holiday soon, and should get on with the job at hand, later to be diagnosed all at once with diabetes, high blood pressure, high cholesterol, and glaucoma. It is incredible how far we will overperform before we have unearthed our overperformance mentalities and swapped them for a more regenerative path.

Can you see your own overperformance picture coming into focus a little more? The cultural narratives and mentalities that you picked up along the way? The clearer it gets, the more readily you will be able to weed out what no longer works for you and adopt the regenerative performance practices that we are going to explore in later chapters.

The stories we live in that lead us to chronic strain are indeed an outcome of culture, but, of course, our personalities and personal histories play a big role in overperformance too. In the next chapter, we will look at one aspect of personal history that can particularly amplify overperformance behaviours, and that is the relationship between the performer and trauma. As we explore trauma, I invite you to go slow and be gentle with yourself and your excavated experiences of overperforming. This is a tricky horizon to bring into view and can feel heavy, but our goal here is simply to see if understanding the role trauma plays can add any more colour to your own developing image.

So, if you can, try to suspend your critical judgement and look at the picture with curiosity and compassion, which might mean some emotional regulation and giving yourself a breather here and there if the topics really hit home for you. Our exploration is purposeful – shedding what doesn't serve you and helping you to meet the moment you find yourself in now with clear eyes and an open heart. Remember, whatever your history, it doesn't have to be your future.

3.

TRAUMA AND THE PERFORMER

When it comes to overperformance and the willingness to ignore your own needs – sometimes for years – in order to keep driving onwards, we absolutely have to look at how much of your time is spent in survival mode, of one kind or another.

When Coping Becomes Overperformance

The link between adverse childhood experiences (ACEs) and performance is well established in the research literature, and kids who have experienced trauma have often been shown to have more trouble with academic achievement, to struggle with learning, attention and engagement in school activities, and reaching educational milestones, which, in part, is because of the impact of ACEs on brain development.[17] Likewise, ACEs have been shown to be strongly associated with emotional and behavioural problems, including depression, anxiety, risk-taking, and difficulty regulating emotions, which can interfere with the ability to succeed in life as both a child and adult. All of these links between childhood trauma and how a person behaves and sees life are responses, and we can easily see how they might cause suffering and difficulty.

But there is another link between ACEs or trauma and how a person behaves: for some people, negative childhood experiences actually build resilience. How often have you heard someone describe a hard time as "character building"? These people know how to bounce back, they might be able to rally teammates or friends and show the way, and they trust that they can get through most things and "tough it out". If it doesn't kill you, it makes you stronger, right? Not entirely. When resilience-built-out-of-trauma works in a person's favour, they have usually had strong, targeted, ongoing social support and help to make meaning of their experiences and decide how they want to use it positively in their life. It's a fine balance, which can often spill over into do-or-die approaches that end up in exhaustion and isolation.

Undoubtedly, a large percentage of the very top performers I have worked with across different fields carry some deep pain, and some of them use it as fuel. They can do things that seem unfathomable to the next person, like tolerating physical distress or shutting out the world in order to achieve a mighty goal. The way I see this, though, is that childhood trauma really informs how much strain you can and will tolerate, because you are effectively pretty well-practised at being in survival mode. Survival mode is do-or-die mode. It is literally the sense that you will end if you don't escape/succeed at getting beyond the problem. And it's hard to ever feel that you are far enough beyond the problem to be safe. It is too much for a child to handle and so they learn coping-as-surviving, and they don't necessarily learn coping-as-thriving. Shutting out the world in order to achieve may become their default mode.

By no means does being in long-term survival mode mean that you feel burgeoning panic at all times or that you are always frantic. In fact, people with "trauma imprints" (strong and lasting mental learnings that mean that your response to events and sensations of today are heavily influenced by previous traumatic experiences), can seem like the calmest and most capable in the room in a crisis – straight-faced, stealthy, and unflinching; this is their home ground after all. What it does mean is that they are expending massive amounts of energy all the time, and it might be really, really hard to put it all down and rest. If this is you, you might recognise yourself in some of the examples in this chapter and the next.

And so, we can see that a person who has a trauma imprint can be really good at ignoring their own needs and staying in that perform-at-all-costs mode – not just in a moment of crisis, but as a way of getting through life. You get the job done, sometimes better than the next person, because you know how to get through pain and strain and stress. The problem is that your methods were developed for crisis, and as a child with a child's understanding and needs. As an adult, that mode of operation can cost you dearly in terms of your mental, emotional, spiritual, and physical health. That mode of operation becomes who you think you are. And however good your performances are, I suspect that you are dragging around way more weight than you need to – because there are better options for doing well and staying whole.

It is possible to choose when to hustle without becoming numb to your feelings and needs. And it is possible to perform with the kind of intensity that you can recover from. The clearer your personal overperformance picture becomes, the easier it will be to become a regenerative performer in future. That is where you, and that not-insignificant amount of courage you already have to be considering such a shift, are heading.

What Do We Mean by Trauma?

We know so much more about trauma now than we did even 15 years ago. We know that it isn't just about the traumatic event or events, but that it is about the internal wound and psychological impact that results. Trauma is the current imprint of past pain, shock, or fear (especially from childhood) that lives inside a person and affects how they see and experience the world.

Renowned addictions and trauma specialist Dr Gabor Maté uses the Greek origin of the word trauma (meaning "wound") to emphasise this point.[18] We think of a wound as healed when we can no longer see visible scars on the surface, but not everything that is an injury is visible. It is how we cope with trauma, large and small, that shapes our personality, our ways of coping with and facing the world.

Dr Maté makes the distinction between "small-t trauma", which includes feeling neglect, emotional abandonment, or lack of love, and "capital-T Trauma", which includes abuse, facing depravity, violence, war, loss, and loss of hope. We can readily relate to capital-T Trauma when we see it and understand the gravity it may have on a person's life experiences. But small-t trauma can be harder to spot at first. It becomes part of a person's way of being, things we associate with their personality and character, but which are actually wounds.

The large and small traumas we travel through are root origins of the addictions and frayed, strained mental health we might experience later in life. This can include addiction to work, addiction to winning, and addiction to endless doing.

It's always worth remembering that trauma is a subjective experience, and how a person absorbs trauma is dependent on many factors, including their personalities, cultural setting, support systems, how much emotional and physical resource they have available at the time, and, as outlined previously, how they are able to make sense of what happened. What we do know is that when a person is left alone and isolated to sense-make and cope, the trauma is likely to stay hidden behind a wall of shame and uneasiness. Unhealed trauma is a form of desolation, an emptiness and loneliness that can continually seep into and change the colour of a life. Until, that is, we can come back to ourselves, to each other, and to the web of life.

Let's now look at a few common examples of how childhood trauma shows up as overperformance in later life. If you recognise yourself in any of this, acknowledge what you are feeling – don't squash it this time. Perhaps put one hand on your chest and the other on your belly and state the feeling quietly and clearly to yourself. Let it breathe, as you breathe. The care for yourself and permission to feel is so important in this journey. When you give yourself permission to feel – whether that might be anger or sadness, fear, pain, resentment or resistance, pride or protection, to name but a few examples – you are way closer to giving permission to do it differently in future.

Emotional numbing

If you are emotionally numbing, you might feel like you are watching life from behind a sheet of glass, slightly removed from reality, not quite there. You might have trouble really feeling joy when something amazing happens, and equally being able to feel big emotions like grief for any sustained amount of time when you lose someone. Why? Because when you were a kid, some of the emotions you felt were just too big or unwelcome, and so you learned to shut them down. If you were told to be quiet if you cried or expressed fear, or perhaps that your anger and frustration were "too much", you quickly learned that emotions were not OK. If you got the feeling that there was no space for your emotions in the face of a parent's overwhelm, you likely learned to anaesthetise your feelings. You learned to become numb – a useful survival technique then, but something that may prevent you from wholebeing as you mature.

If this is you, as an adult, you may stay in toxic relationships for way too long; you might turn up for work when you are unwell, ignore injuries, or work through periods of personal loss or pain without even mentioning it. You may drift into substance misuse or abuse, which can range from that necessary glass or three of wine at night to a quiet and creeping addiction to painkillers – anything to deaden the feelings.

Parentification

The term parentification means becoming a caregiver too soon, usually when you were a child yourself. This can happen if your parents were unable to be present physically or emotionally, and so you decided (and sometimes were told) that looking after everyone was your job. You may have been the "responsible one" growing up, the helper, the emotional support, the peacemaker, the pleaser. It may have earned you credit as a kid and, indeed, it may still earn you credit as an adult who takes on everyone else's burdens, rescues people, and is regarded as the "grown-up" in the group. If so, it's likely that you learned to ignore your own needs along the way.

Kids who have to act like adults too early often struggle with boundaries and burnout later on in life. They find it hard to rest, or feel selfish when they take some time to look after themselves. In later life, this is the person who says yes when they are already triple-parked on tasks. This is the person who somehow seeks to take on even more when they are already overwhelmed and stressed, because they feel somehow at home in the chaos. This is the person who puts themself into discomfort and harbours secret resentment, but cannot say no.

Fear of being vulnerable

If as a child you experienced rejection or mocking when you asked for help or expressed hard feelings, when you showed or said that you didn't feel safe, or when something went wrong and you needed care, you likely decided that it was a bad idea to show vulnerability or ask for help again. Similarly, if there was no response to your needs when you showed them, if your caregiver repeatedly "shushed" you, closed you down, or turned away, you likely decided that needs were not cool. These types of responses bring shame, and a child doesn't know what to do with that other than turn it in on themself and blame themself for speaking up when they shouldn't have. Shame puts down deep roots in the psyche, preventing you from wanting to speak up for yourself or for your needs in future – or not feeling stable and calm when you do.

As an adult, a person who fears being vulnerable is less likely to reach for opportunities despite their talents, less likely to call out practices in a workplace or in a relationship that are damaging, and less likely to ask for support when they need it. A person who doesn't want to be exposed might avoid admitting problems such as financial difficulties, learning difficulties, or health issues until they feel out of hand and overwhelming.

Perfectionism

If you learned as a child that the "real you" who was still learning and growing and testing and practising, the one who made mistakes and got things wrong, who made poor choices while they worked out what good choices were and who sometimes said and did annoying things – if you learned that they were not acceptable and not really lovable, you might have decided that it wasn't safe to let them out "in public". The alternative that you created may have been a "perfect" kid; one who did not risk rejection again and avoided the searing pain of not feeling worthy – in a classroom, in a home, in a friendship group. That "perfect" kid needed to be vigilant and tight, no margin for error, because the risk of being shamed was too high. The "real you" had to remain hidden with their confusion, their sadness, their grief, and maybe their rage.

This is often the first time a child puts on an overperformance mask. As an adult, that mask stays firmly on. This person might feel uneasy if they do not incessantly check their mail and their socials, because they cannot be out of the loop or tolerate the feeling of being behind. This is the chronic midnight worker, the person who seeks to control as many aspects of their life as possible, from their weight to their health to their achievements and their friendships, barely daring to take a breath in between.

There are, of course, many other manifestations of trauma, but perhaps you are getting the picture: the overperformer in all of us might have a little trouble letting go.

Overperformance, Trauma, and Control

I want to emphasise the point that while it is not inevitable that a person who chronically overperforms has experienced some trauma in their lives, in my years working with performers of all kinds, I can attest to a strong anecdotal link at the very least. What I see is that people who often feel or felt, to some degree, unsafe or unloved, also often feel that they have to prove their very worth in extreme ways. A person who has felt unloved or conditionally loved, for instance, not only walks into the room carrying that wound, they may be likely to behave in ways that keep the cycle of fear and control in their mind going. They might take the "lone wolf" position; resisting closeness, integration, help or care (for fear of more pain), and standing away from the pack, while at the same time silently driving themselves into the ground trying to seem appealing, desperate to be accepted and invited in, needing praise and acknowledgement, but not trusting or believing it when it comes, because they fundamentally don't think they are really lovable in the first place – and if they don't control the circumstances, someone else might work that out too.

For one of my clients, Adeye, it looked like this:

> My parents were strict. Strict about how I looked, who I hung out with, and what my grades were at school. If I had less than perfect results on schoolwork, it would go quiet around the dinner table and the smell of disappointment was intense. I respect them a lot, but I don't think I had what I would call a close relationship with them because I was always so careful around them. And the love was undoubtedly conditional. If I didn't succeed at something, which was rare, there would be a consequence – which usually meant a cancellation of some social connection I cared about at age 5 or 15, or a withdrawal of love in another way – especially not

letting me play football, which was my outlet, but which they thought was not something that "respectable" girls did.

I remember my mother wouldn't look at me, and my father would express his disappointment more directly with words, like "Failure is not acceptable in this family, Adeye" or "You should show your mother more respect for how she raised you than coming home with grades like this/than wearing that/than parading your body around a football field." To be clear, the "failed" grade would be an A-.

Honestly, I thought that it was quite funny in a way, and a lot of my friends had the same deal; we laughed about it. I didn't recognise then how much it sunk into me. But I think two things started to happen in that time that really shaped me or changed me. One was that I started to feel very competitive about everything. Not like passionately competing and enjoying myself, but fearfully competing. It was like zero-sum competing, me or you, win or die. It was a negative force that made me constantly anxious although no one knew that, and there wasn't anything that I didn't compete over, which was really bad for friendships. I think I felt that if I was "ahead" all of the time, I was out of reach of criticism. Unassailable.

The other thing that happened was that I got really "jumpy" mentally and emotionally. I couldn't be light. I was tense and defensive often and I behaved like everything was a judgement of me in some way or me judging others. It was pretty shitty. It must have been hard to be around me. Then Covid hit and I was forced into isolation at home for what felt like 100 years. My father's income was slashed as a self-employed person, and the stress in the house was sky high, mostly about how people would see us rather than any real material problems, and I got the brunt of that stress for some reason. At the same time, I started to feel this impending sense of doom, of not knowing how to think about the future because absolutely everything felt up in the air and uncertain; climate change, global war, pandemics. And I think I felt trapped, like I might never break away.

I was just so relieved to get a graduate job at a well-known global media firm as Covid eased its grip. I literally showed up on day one with a Terminator mentality, I was not going to let anything stop me from succeeding. All my A-student training, my compliance and rigidity, and this awful, aggressive competitiveness that had developed got deployed. I thought at the time that I was loving the place, even though I never saw daylight or a football and barely slept. It allowed me to be relentless and temporarily "safe" and probably to just avoid all feelings. At least they fed me and I could get my washing done at work. I was like Terminator – a cyborg!

I had experienced stomach issues throughout my teenage years, but never really paid much attention, except for one big, awful flare-up where my mother got me medically tested and they diagnosed irritable bowel syndrome, which felt vague and not like something I could fix. I felt like she was angry. I felt like this condition was disappointing her. We never spoke about it again once we left the doctor's office. Eighteen months into working at the company, though, my flare-ups were horrible, debilitating, and exhausting. They started happening very regularly and I was in a world of discomfort, getting grumpier and angrier at myself by the day, but still not saying anything, not doing anything about it, or not even stopping. Until I literally had to stop because I broke down and couldn't function. Then came the shame, then the sadness. I held that sadness back for my whole life, held it in my gut. That's the one I couldn't face.

In his seminal book *The Body Keeps the Score*, psychiatrist Bessel van der Kolk explains that the urgent work of the brain after trauma is to suppress it, through diminishing, denying, or self-blaming.[19]

His position is that this is a method used to avoid being abandoned or ostracised, because noticing or facing the pain might involve recognising other people's parts in our pain, and that might just feel too risky to our survival at some level. We cannot always face the real source of our pain, especially if it is feeling unloved or unwanted by people who we love and want – that feels too big. It feels like it might swallow us whole, and so we store it or "share it" in other ways. Did you notice how Adeye laughed off her lack of love with her friends? And did you notice how she was getting angry at herself for not being able to continue in cyborg mode as she became ill?

Whatever instructions our minds throw out, telling us to ignore and repress our feelings, our body does not forget; it keeps a record in its very structure and cellular activity, as if we stay in this suspended state, frozen in time, as teacher and trauma expert Thomas Hübl says, until we start to heal.[20]

Our body feels threat well before our mind gets involved and, actually, we can feel threat even if we do not cognitively compute that there is a threat present. Take, for example, something simple like having a tattoo or a small elective surgery that you have given full permission for and willingly submitted yourself to. Logically, you know that there is no threat and that any discomfort will be minimal, purposeful, and temporary, but your body responds to the prolonged "infringement" as if it were real and present danger and floods you with biochemical responses that leave you exhausted for a couple of days afterwards, even in such a small "vignette" of threat. Imagine how that imprint is laid in a young person who senses threat regularly and has no way of processing it or making sense of it.

But when we do recognise that we are not safe, and we keep ignoring what we feel in order to keep active, to keep running, and to keep overperforming, we are at a heightened risk of hitting a disease state eventually, something which Dr Maté associates with the immune and inflammatory responses in the body.[21]

An overwhelmed nervous system can lead to physiological changes, such as a recalibration of the brain's alarm system. Usually, this system turns us on to high alert, vigilance, fear, and oversensitivity to real danger signals. But feeling abandoned, emotionally unsafe, neglected, or unlovable as a child are all enough to overwhelm the nervous system, creating states of chronic hyper-arousal or dysregulation that can endure and keep that brain alarm system on 24/7.

Our relationships evoke intensity of all kinds, and there are only so many ways the body can manifest that intensity. For Adeye, it showed up as competitiveness and as inflammation in her digestive system. An overwhelmed nervous system can also increase stress hormones, which get stored in the muscles and leave us in a regular cortisol fog. Perhaps you can recognise some of these symptoms of overwhelm in yourself?

- Irritability, reactivity, and mood swings
- Difficulty concentrating and restlessness
- Avoidance of tasks
- Feeling sluggish, confused, or unable to recall details
- Sleep disturbances
- Muscle tension especially in the jaw, neck, and back
- Headaches
- Digestive distress and appetite changes
- Heart palpitations
- Feelings of panic
- Body temperature fluctuations
- Oversensitivity to loud noises, touch, or bright lights

How often do you shrug these things off as random, or "just a big week/month/year"?

Overperformance, Trauma, and Threat

It was in this kind of trauma-based fog and confused signalling that my client Robyn found her way to burnout in a new work environment that she knew was toxic within a week of being there. She had jubilantly joined a sports media organisation as an executive, keen to lead some big changes in the way things were done. What she found was a truly old-school power-and-ego-dominated culture; an "insiders" club' with untouchable bullies, who did not intend to make room for her.

Robyn was a person who presented as mature and capable, a leader. But she had experienced her share of small-t trauma and, for her, it played out as closing down her feelings and trying harder and harder to prove her worth – well and truly in an overperformance zone.

This is how she describes what happened for her:

> *My ability to dissociate from my experiences was really dangerously exacerbated within that environment. I was so separated from my feelings, my own thoughts, my physical reality, and my psychological reality, that I was getting very, very lost – but that was a journey that went way, way back into origins.*
>
> *From a very young age, I had learned not to have needs and desires. And so when people would ask me, "Do you want a snack, are you hungry?", as a kid, I would say, "I don't mind". Or maybe they'd ask, "Would you like this flavour or that flavour?" and I'd say, "I don't mind". I vividly recall going out for pizza with one of my very best friends in our early 20s – we were going to share a pizza and she said to me, "What flavour would you like on our shared pizza?" and I said, "I don't mind" and she said, "Hey, you must mind, you must have a preference, you must know. Otherwise everyone else will decide for you." The truth was I didn't know. It might seem like a crazy example, but you can become so divorced from your own wishes and wants, in case they cause disappointment, that you genuinely don't even know what they are.*
>
> *I think that is probably a really common experience for lots of people. Especially women and girls who have this idea that our needs should be put aside for others, and our desires might*

not be "appropriate" or you might be too demanding or too difficult and that we should be afraid of the word "No" as well. It makes me think a lot about people who have been through sexual violence or any other kind of violent trauma, who often report feeling separated and disassociated from their bodies while they watch whatever is happening, happen. There is something in that, a kind of split. For me, that ability to split off just came back fully and really strongly in that work environment; I was very much dissociated by the end. It just made me feel so tense and incompetent and debilitated and weak. I felt constantly threatened. I was really just a shell of myself at that point.

Why did I stay? Partly because of the care and concern I had for others who experience this and who were not senior leaders, who had less protection than I did. I had a heavy sense of responsibility to stick it out and take the bow and arrows and break through — I guess to be a bit of a martyr really. I also felt that they wouldn't get to my core, but that was wrong, they did. My core was less protected than I thought, as I found out when I crashed and burned out. Also, I didn't want to lose or be a loser. I think I felt that only if I was victorious would they be able to see value. And victory looked like resilience and never quitting, whatever the cost.

In Robyn's case, her felt experience of being resisted and closed-out led her to double-down and try to demonstrate that she was worthy. At the same time, she had quickly stopped feeling psychologically safe, and couldn't seem to get any acknowledgement or traction with her boss that things were awry and the behaviour of her adult peers was unacceptable — something that may have helped her to cope without being triggered by her own trauma. In the absence of that, her response was to try to suppress her feelings and pretend she was OK. You could say that she got "stuck" or frozen in her state of threat, her nervous system rarely out of defence mode.

Robyn was becoming increasingly depleted, overworking and over-analysing daily to try to find a safe foothold, scanning her environment for cues and clues about how to be accepted. We all need cues of safety in order to relax. Cues can include subtle things like sounds and movements that do not signal to our brain that we are in a prey–predator situation. So, when a person like Robyn might hear, "It's all fine, keep going, nothing to see here..." while simultaneously experiencing danger signals like raised voices, shouting, frowning, tutting faces with raised eyebrows, side glances exchanged between colleagues when she spoke, being left off meeting invites or excluded from social events, and hearing poisonous judgement and dismissal of other colleagues disguised as banter, the overwhelming experience was one of subversive threat.

We live in a world where we believe that what we say is the most important thing, but our bodies don't prioritise linguistics, they prioritise intonation, energy, and feel. What Robyn could feel was the intensity of wiry, jumpy, aggressive, staticky, stuck, egoic, scared, inauthentic energy directed at her, and there was no way she could stay well and whole in that environment. Her own history of small-t trauma magnified the effects.

When we are made to feel excluded, rejected, unwelcome, isolated, and outside the group, we feel threat. This is unpleasant on any given day, but when there is old, stored trauma, which is tremendously common, we can also be easily triggered into strong visceral responses that are overwhelming, confusing, and may feel "outsized" to the situation or at odds with our rational take on the situation or our stated intentions.

The Need to Connect

The thing is, connecting to others is not just a nice-to-have for us humans. Connectedness is a biological imperative; we unequivocally need others in order to flourish as social animals. Sure, we can survive (as adults) if we are lonely and isolated for extended periods, but we cannot feel whole or thrive. From a neurobiological perspective, connectedness functions as a kind of love code, a way of understanding that things are OK and we can relax. You can be a committed introvert who relishes a bit of solitude (like me) and still know that you are part of a web of connections in order to feel truly OK.

Reciprocity and co-regulation are also biological imperatives, not nice-to-haves. Reciprocity means mutual exchange, the sense of doing things in relationship to each other, with each other, for each other, and, in some form, cooperating with each other. It's an essential source of meaning in human life. Co-regulation means fostering a sense of stability and well-being by being around others. It can happen directly one-on-one when you snuggle up with your partner – or your dog – on the couch, and it can happen just by coming into a pleasant ambient space like a cafe where other people seem relaxed and open to you being there, even if you never speak or touch. Take the example of walking alone on a dark, empty street to meet some friends – you are subconsciously experiencing some degree of threat until then you turn into a vibrant, well-lit space with lots of people enjoying themselves, and your body releases the tension even before you have seen your friends. You co-regulated in community.

In both of these performer-trauma stories, Adeye and Robyn felt like they had to push on despite pain and suffering in various forms. When a person has a trauma history, immobilisation or staying still can create great vulnerability and, quite literally, feel like a threat to survival. This often translates into workaholic behaviours laced with high anxiety and numbness. The general sentiment is "as long as I keep moving, I can't shut down".

The bottom line is that chronic overperformance is a proxy for not feeling safe in some way. And when a person does not feel safe enough inside to be truly authentic, really honest about how they feel and what they need, they hide, withhold, or "game it".

Recognising this is not a moment to call yourself or anyone else out for bullshitting – if you are masking and overperforming as a result of trauma, you are saying: "I haven't yet learned to trust myself sufficiently to be fully honest in how I show up in the world."

Trauma leaves imprints on our lives in many ways. It makes us hide or hold inauthenticity in great swathes of our existence, and it exhausts us. The term "worn out" feels so pertinent to me in respect to "performer trauma". To be "worn" is to be damaged or shabby from much use, and "out" means to move away from a particular place, perhaps a place of sanctuary or home, or to be distanced from somewhere. To be worn out as a performer is to have grown threadbare from being so far away from the "home" within that you can no longer hold your shape.

By now, as you read, perhaps you have a useful image of how you learned who to be, and how those stories, mentalities, and experiences can link to overperformance. The solid frame around the picture is made up of our collective cultural stories, and the specific details of the picture within the frame are made from your own life and meaning-making. You might not love all of the parts of your overperformance picture; you might even want to reject them. The point of having a real look is that now you can see more clearly what might hook you into doing more, staying small, and conforming when you don't want to. You can see more clearly the situations that trigger you into ignoring yourself and behaving in ways that you don't much like. And this is also the point where you can start to acknowledge that your existing picture is not inevitable, so if you can feel the rumbling of your will to adjust it for the better, for your future, just know that you are stepping in the right direction, and again, trust your courage and listen to your heart and gut as we travel.

In Part 2, we'll look at how overperformance in different areas of your life – not just work – leaves you with the psychological heartburn that I hope to help you ease in the rest of this book.

PART 2.

OVERPERFORMANCE AND ITS CONSEQUENCES

Now that you have a good picture of what drives us to overperform, it's time to take a deeper look at overperformance itself. You will see where overperformance starts to become a problem; when it becomes chronic and when it becomes hard to work out where the real you stops and the well-trained overperformer in you takes the reins.

You will see that it shows up in surprising places, and just how embedded in your ways of being it might be. You will also get a glimpse of the kind of havoc it can wreak if it goes unchecked. My objective in this section is to help you to consider where in your own life you might be overperforming. For you, it might begin with a moment of feeling off-track and the choice to stop and listen inwardly to what you are feeling and noticing. If you have picked up this book because you are already feeling burnt out, my hope is that this part can help you to see that your discomfort might not be something to fix so that you can "get back to it", but a doorway to something deeper, something truer in you, and that grief and disorientation that you feel are, in fact, natural responses to collapsing ways of being.

As you read, keep listening to the thread of life and let it guide the way.

4.

WAYS WE OVERPERFORM

Chronic overperformance is not knowing how to be faithful to yourself anymore, especially to your feelings. When this happens, we try to respond to the dis-ease it creates with something we are really familiar with, and really good at: performing. As we have explored, performing itself is fabulous, desirable, and necessary, but many of you may find yourself being performative – doing what you think you ought to be doing or what you are expected to be doing – because you have lost sight of what feels true and natural for you. You might also find yourself stretching your limits or your boundaries and over-reaching, at a high cost to yourself. We all do it, at least in some areas of our lives. And, of course, it's not the end of the world to be performative on occasion or to overstretch here and there, but when it starts to be the way you are consistently, it can really erode your sense of self, your inner peace, and your wholebeing as a person. I believe that chronic overperformance is an underexplored, silent chaos-creator, and if you can start to recognise the ways you might be playing into it in your own life, you can put yourself in a position to change it too.

So, how do you know if you're doing it? When people are perennial overperformers, they tend to do these things:

- **Self-sacrifice:** A significant and regular willingness to compromise and ignore personal well-being including base physical, social, and psychological needs in order to achieve or attain an external goal.
- **Masking:** Consciously or unconsciously covering, hiding, denying, or pretending in order to fit the perceived expectations of others, feel safe, or avoid their own or others' negative emotions. This is especially true of covering stress and strain.
- **Psychological scrolling:** Endlessly "scrolling" their personhood and environment to see how they compare, where the gaps are, what ought to be better, what might happen next, and what else should they be aware of or comparing to.
- **Side-thinking:** Rarely maintaining presence with what they are doing or who they are with, without starting a "new thread", a new list, opening a new mental tab, picking up their phone, checking out who else is around, or running another script.
- **Having a fantasy finish line:** Assuming that everything about their overperformance will change once they have "moved the needle" far enough through their own effort, attainment, or behaviour.
- **Having a compelling story about why it's needed:** A long-held narrative or mentality that runs deep, may be privately held, and justifies or rationalises the overperformance behaviour.

This is not just about how you work. Chronic overperformance can show up in many places in your life. We think of something like burnout – a dramatic end result of chronic overperformance – as a workplace issue because that's what gets measured and that's where we can see it collectively, but it is happening in our homes and our schools and our relationships too. Being an overperformer shows up in our habits, what we can and cannot engage with, what we prioritise and protect.

I believe that there are three places where we can see overperformance that are especially relatable, and they are work, love, and the way we look.

Overworking

Work in our contemporary culture is often an endurance event; a quantity proposition. And a workaholic, despite being regularly celebrated, will likely die before an alcoholic, according to burnout researcher Christina Maslach.[22]

The raft of physical and mental health consequences of overwork are no small thing. The World Health Organization and the International Labour Organization suggest that each year, three quarters of a million people are dying from coronary heart disease and stroke related to working long hours.[23] A Finnish study of 603,000 people in Europe, the US, and Australia in 2015 showed that people who work more than 55 hours a week doubled their risk of heart attacks and increased their risk of a stroke by a third.[24] Since 1987 there has even been a term for it in Japan: *karoshi* (death by overwork), and official estimates over the last few years put *karoshi* levels at 2,300 deaths per year. However, the National Defense Council for Victims of Karoshi estimate that numbers could be as high as 10,000 per year in reality. For families of *karoshi* victims to receive official compensation and benefits, the worker must have a track record of doing more than 100 hours per week over an extended period.[25]

But it's the un-health that comes before illness or death that so many of us also recognise: the crisis mindset, irritability, never-ending sense of urgency, flashes of temper, pending panic, guilt, grating anxiety, anger, disappointment, listlessness, and foggy thinking. It's the extremes of feeling like you're either dragging around an extra 20 kg in exhaustion or you're getting the late-night/ early-morning caffeinated frazzle that distorts your physical and mental essence but lets you get shit done. It's the skipping lunch and running late, and it's the inability to come back to some kind of balance for very long at all. Overwork sucks the dynamism and genuine confidence out of you. It's impossible to find the real self-assurance that comes from a quiet inward gaze if you are constantly living with fractured attention.

Sometimes, overworking just seems needed and we get through it for a moment – a tough period or a hump. For overworking to tip into chronic overperformance, it needs to be both resistant to change and connected to the cultural narratives we met in Chapter 1 and the personal performance mentalities from Chapter 2 – those stories about yourself that sit deep in your psyche.

"Chronic" in this context means being stuck in overdrive for the long term. Chronic means it doesn't stop. When you get into this space, you might feel that you have to protect or hoard the energy that you have left in order to get through your life. That might mean that you feel the need to close down all else and become hyper-focused on performing, including any complaints or signals from your body or perhaps the people closest to you. You stay hyper-responsive to demands and "need-to-do" messages from your mind at all hours, and say "Yes" when you definitely mean "Oh God, no".

The narrative that tips plain old overwork into overperformance is the narrative of optimisation, the story of necessary, endless productivity that requires visible and invisible sacrifices and underpins the oft-skewed psychological contract between employer and employee, a contract that can say, "In exchange for money, status, and belonging, you will *give it all* for our results." When this is coupled with the narrative of more, which says, "You need more" and the exceptionalism narrative that says, "You can be and should be the exception", we are locked in. Add to that a mentality such as "one shot at your potential" or "once I cross the line", and you can see the potent pull to push on regardless.

A former client of mine, a senior sports executive in her late 30s, recently got to feel the full force of overperforming as a new, first-time mum working in her "dream club". Before she had a child, she describes herself as a classic overworking, midnight-Slack-channel-using, liquid-food-inhaling, airport-check-in-staff-know-my-first-name, running-on-fumes kind of woman who mostly felt like she was heading in the right direction career-wise. She acknowledges that she wilfully ignored her growing exhaustion, her new husband, her family and circle of friends, her polycystic ovary issues because, well … *this was it* … the big opportunity, and she needed to do whatever it took to *make it* in this role. She thought that this was a high-performance attitude: never quit. She had been promoted twice in her tenure and was in the "big job", as she described it, when she fell pregnant, earlier than she had planned. A cascade of mixed feelings filled her heart and mind at the news, but being a parent was part of her imagined future and she believed she could make it all work.

Through the pregnancy, she maintained the same intensity and pace, but she also volunteered for more responsibility when a colleague left and someone needed to "double job" until his replacement was hired. She described feeling increasingly desperate to prove that being a mum would not change her results or commitment. She took as many flights, worked as many nights and weekends, and, despite feeling increasingly depleted, she resisted the concerned enquiries of her colleagues and family and revelled in the psychological applause of her bosses: "She's a machine." Reluctantly, she went on maternity leave at eight-and-a-half months with a promise to be back within six weeks – for the club football finals – and by the time she gave birth, she was worn out. And then, of course, came arguably the biggest possible transition and performance a person ever experiences in their lives: becoming responsible for a small, completely dependent human baby who has zero interest in the finals.

Wow did I get a wake-up call. This was not something to start while tired and out of touch with yourself and your partner. Within three or four weeks, I was a wreck, but everyone said that they were a wreck at first too, so I pushed on, tried to plan my way through it, find an operational rhythm for work and baby, do it like I did everything else. I can laugh at that now. But I started to feel something else, something I can only describe as a sort of "fraying" of my sense of myself. I noticed how anxious I got when I was out of the loop at work, and I felt like I was pretending in all areas of my life. Who was I? What was I doing and why? Did anyone even care? I realised I felt unsafe, unprotected if I wasn't giving 110 per cent. And then came burnout…

We are trained to believe that going above and beyond will be the thing that moves the needle towards achieving our goals and that if all of us do this at all times, we will all succeed. But does the relentless focus on getting ahead at work through effort and hustle really work? For whom? You, or the organisational bottom line? You, or the scoreboard? You today, or that imaginary future self who has crossed the finish line and is having a margarita in a hammock in an imagined forever-paradise?

What is it that you compromise to be that chronic workplace overperformer? The good health that lets you show up each day and participate in your craft? Your relationships outside of work? Your ability to approach something spaciously and creatively rather than quickly? Your ability to grow, expand, and deepen in other ways that might actually inspire your work? Your sense of adventure or playfulness? The feeling of having enough time to appreciate yourself or the work you do? The room to notice when your passions have shifted, lifted, or faded? These can feel like things you have to trade-off to get ahead. I think they are more like a false economy in your psychology – what feels like an investment in the short term is, in fact, way too much wasted expenditure in the end, and the end is no time to start rethinking how you want to live.

In the meantime, we find ourselves in a culture that is hostile to rest. Rest is considered indulgent, luxurious, maybe a bit lazy in a culture where overperformance is socially and culturally sanctioned and celebrated. This is market-mind propaganda designed to keep that vigilant productivity machine turning at all costs, extracting overperformance in exchange for your wholebeing. You are not required to comply. As the brilliant poet Tricia Hersey says, "rest is resistance".[26]

In a compelling conversation with Dr Rangan Chatterjee, Dr Maté shared a moving reflection on his life as an overworker and the role of rest and play:

> I wish I hadn't worked so hard. When you are driven to work too hard, you actually ignore what matters. And what matters is what you were telling me last night, about how every summer you take a bunch of weeks away from your podcast and you just spend time enjoying your kids and your wife and your family. I didn't do that. I always felt that I had to keep working.[27]

Our stories do not see performance as something requiring play, wholeness, renewal, or regeneration – they see it as something requiring sacrifice, discipline, and compliance.

A very accomplished performer I know from the world of media shared her thoughts on how she learned to be an overworker and an overperformer. What is especially notable in her story is the role that trauma played in her willingness to bend herself out of shape until she crashed and burned – as we explored in the last chapter. Her good-girl smile eventually started to hurt her jaw. The tension wrapped around her chest made it hard for her to fully exhale. She explained:

I think, from early on in my life, I felt I had to find a way to exist that was safe and where I wouldn't step on trip wires or cause anyone to explode. I guess I learned to walk on eggshells. I developed something of a "good-girl theory" that basically said that if we can just be perfect enough, perform well enough, and delight people enough, if we can be good all the time, irrefutably, undeniably good, the best, then we will be protected from hurt, and we will be protected from harm. I took this straight into my career and, in that world, it meant overworking, always saying yes, being the trusted one, and leaning in until I couldn't lean anymore without toppling.

I also see how deep-rooted her beliefs were that she could "effort" and prove her way out of a rough situation while hiding her pain:

I guess so many of us wear a mask in pursuit of success or achievement and in order to stay "inside the circle" at work. As a performer, I would tread the boards and play the game brilliantly, even when I secretly eye-rolled or cringed or felt overwhelmed by things, and, quite honestly, I felt like I could do it forever. I felt like it was normal; the way. But, ultimately, there comes a point where you are juggling so many balls that you simply can't sustain the performance anymore. I think that we are taught from school that you are supposed to climb the ladder with no stepping off or stepping down, and the key to climbing was sacrifice – you just had to tolerate a lot to be climbing. Until I couldn't pretend anymore. For me, everything slowly kind of melted and slipped or corroded, like my mind was too tightly wound or something. I could not give all of myself to somebody else's chase for results anymore; it was too lonely. My body and mind just said no.

By the time she left the organisation, she was well and truly out of fuel. She had tried herself into burnout in a place that seemed unwilling to meet her trying in good faith. Unwilling to accept the adrenal fatigue that her body was signalling through constricted lungs and a raspy throat or the loss of her identity that her shaky voice hinted at, she "melted". It was an unconscious survival mechanism.

This executive is whip-smart, resourceful, and has "all the gold stars" on her résumé, but none of that provided protection from the consequences of chronic overperformance in an environment where her values were not aligned, and her response was to prove that she wasn't a quitter.

Over-loving

It's fair to say that the world needs a whole lot more love right at the minute, and the idea that there can be ways that we love too much might seem illogical. "How can we overperform at love?" you might ask. We easily recognise overperformance at work, but over-loving might feel harder to see. It is about having so much need and fear tied up in your love relationships that you can't allow yourself to be in your natural state in case it is not enough, and so you love in a performative way – you put your mask on and, again, bend yourself out of shape to get your needs met and meet the needs you think your loved one has of you... Like my client with the famous boyfriend in Chapter 2 who literally couldn't show her natural face.

Loving someone means, among other things, that you respect each other's boundaries. Over-loving means that you dismantle those boundaries, stop taking care of yourself, and do everything for another person in order to make them happy and ensure you are safe in the knowledge that no stone was left unturned in your efforts to be a great partner in the relationship. This is a form of overperformance.

Idealistically, love doesn't have much to do with performance – we want to see it as a pure, organic, naturally occurring phenomenon, not something that gets caught up in the sketchy world of status, gains, or perfection. Love has a reputation to uphold as the one true soul-soothe after all. Sometimes, though, the cultural narratives that underpin our ways of loving are also the same cultural narratives that drive us in the rest of our performances: separateness, exceptionalism, optimisation, and always needing more.

When the narrative of separateness is part of how we love, we might feel that our intimate relationships can be moulded to the shape that we see fit and not follow the laws of change that the rest of nature follows – they should be the way that we (and popular culture) decree. Whatever our age, our stage, our circumstances, our love relationships should measure up to the highest cultural standards of all. This can mean that we are not so great at accepting change or diversity in a partner. Perhaps that includes unspoken expectations about how stable things ought to stay, how faithful our bodily and psychological energies of desire and yearning will be, and how true to the hormone-soaked moment of commitment we will be until death do we part. This kind of narrative doesn't always help us to "be natural" in relationships.

If we better recognised ourselves as *within* nature, rather than a witness to it, we might consider whether we are doing OK at growing, changing, and regenerating together, rather than repeating the patterns, habits, and expectations we started with, because nothing alive stays the same forever. Consider when you last really looked at whether there is still sufficient diversity in the life you share with your partner, or has the love-niche actually become smaller and more contained, a space that feels a little too tight for the way you have changed? This happens, in friendships too, and it can be a brilliant moment to recognise the need to regenerate or reinvigorate. But, often, what happens instead is that we deny the change and find ourselves overperforming a version of the relationships that we have outgrown. Imagine the water nymph we spoke about in the Introduction pretending it wasn't really a dragonfly and that it might instead force itself to stay as it was! Only humans believe their force of will can override what is natural.

Assuming that we can and should override the natural changes in our inner landscapes may leave us performing (overperforming) a version of our earlier selves when, really, it's far from the grief, sadness, or stuckness that we feel.

Can you recognise in your own life places where cultural expectations have dictated your approach to a love relationship? Places where you might have felt torn or constrained but not acted to change it, because you believe that you ought to be able to rise above and override what you *feel* and rationally, mentally work things through to a sensible outcome?

A former client of mine described his experience of finding himself stuck in a moment in time and overperforming in his relationship:

> *I look back now and realise that my wife started out by what I think is called "love-bombing" me. She was a lively person with her own means and she seemed to me to be very independent-minded. In our first six months together, she did all sorts of things that were over the top, but also delightful and seemingly very generous, thoughtful and loving. For example, she booked surprise weekend trips to Prague and Paris, booked a VIP box for me and four mates at an international rugby match I was dying to see, bought me endless gifts, encouraged me to spend more and more time at her place, and greeted me with home-cooked food and a glass of wine at the end of the day.*
>
> *She sort of really looked out for me and made me feel great. She declared her love for me within weeks really, and texted me all sorts of things that made me blush at work all day long. I guess I was pretty intense with the attention I*

lavished on her then too; it was like a perfect romantic movie with roles played by actors. She said she wanted a partner who was comfortable to be truly himself and that we could have the kind of honest relationship that really worked for independent, grown adults, rather than the cloistered, scary, possessive types of relationships I had encountered before.

I am not a particularly spontaneous person, but it all went very fast and I found myself getting married within 12 months. It was like a switch flicked 12 months after that, when we actually exhaled and the intensity dropped off and we were "just normal". The daytime texts became more like demands laced with disappointment and entitlement, and I felt increasingly like I did not have much room to move. It made me anxious. I felt constantly like I wasn't meeting expectations and I needed to up my game. I was taking care of everything in her life in order to get the feeling back, literally like an employee trying to get a good performance review. It was dizzying. Now, I think we both feel like we have been taken advantage of and I'm full of resentment. It's stalemate and neither of us are happy.

This client's story is also an example of the narrative of exceptionalism, because, as a couple, they were in the territory of chasing specialness, perfection, and being extra-ordinary, different to the rest. Exceptionalism can be seen in love relationships when the desire to be "The One" creates a particular kind of performative over-investment, manifesting in a person making their partner the absolute centre of their universe to the point they actually forget what fills their own cup. Right here is where we can lose our boundaries and standards, and find ourselves overperforming the role of adored, most-special lover and partner, and unable to face even the smallest of challenges or disturbances in the relationship, in case it shatters the picture of perfect. It's a chronic kind of inner-

and outer-vigilance that shuts down wholebeing and is smack bang in the realm of overperformance.

Similarly, exceptionalism shows up in other love relationships like parenting, where a parent tries so hard to be perfect – sometimes because it's the opposite of how they were raised – that they completely overperform, abandoning themselves totally to the role and to the ever-expanding, culture-created, and comparison-laden needs of the child. The parent finds themselves unable to just "be" without being extraordinary.

When a parent loves their child greatly but feels that they don't have any emotional resource or calm presence to offer them right now because they themselves are wrung out, being "exceptional" might show up through something like permission-giving (more screen time, yes to the newest, most expensive trainers, yes to the later bedtime, yes to the sugar-laden "sports" drink). It might also show up as a Cirque du Soleil-level third birthday party as a kind of "counter-balancing" of the parenting ledger. This is a road to spiritual exhaustion for the parent, for a partnership, and sometimes for the child, and, critically, it denies the ordinary grace of being, the normalness of feeling over it as a parent, or of needing to just be average today; a moment without judgement.

Like all forms of overperformance, exceptionalism in love requires us to stay blind to reality. It requires us to anaesthetise our feelings and deny some of our experiences. If you are a parent and find yourself in this overperformance cycle, you are the one in need of some love and care.

My gold-stars-good-girl executive client in the story earlier in the chapter burnt out and needed to take a year out to come home to herself. She reflected on how different she felt about herself as a parent after that year:

> *I was thinking while I was washing up today that over the last year I invested a lot in my children. That isn't something that feels easy to say out loud. In "work world" it would*

sound ridiculous to say I invested in my children, and in family or parent world it might sound a bit sanctimonious, maybe a bit too close to the traditional wife archetype. It has changed my life though, and theirs. My overperformance at work had resulted in under-performance elsewhere, and they got the brunt of that.

I think society tells us to treat parenting like a job to be exceptional at – a job that involves a list of endless tasks, and unreasonable small humans to contend with. Sometimes, they will shame you; sometimes, you can boast about them. They are presented as accessories and examples of us doing well, of our own detached performance. I'm being crude, but there is truth in it. Quiet truth. Parenting really, though, for me, is about opening to human connection. Yes, there is drudgery and tasks to do, but the meat of it, the most important part of it is connection. And in that process, we are all nourished. It's beautiful beyond belief.

Overperforming at love can also be linked with the narrative of optimisation. How many relationships do you know where there never seems to be a reprieve from doing? Always a packed agenda, fast-track, go-hard, win-big, goal-oriented, trouble-free, and whistle-stop. The energy of this kind of relationship is improvement energy, productivity energy, proving energy, and "endless renovation" energy, not the soulful energy of sanctuary that comes with the place and space to let go and be free, as you are. The essence of optimisation is that things are not good enough as they are and with effort we can improve them. Of course, all relationships have things that need working on, and all relationships do require massive amounts of effort, but perhaps that effort is the effort of vulnerability, of opening and exploring, rather than the effort of fixing and doing. Perhaps love of all kinds is something that we are supposed to mellow with or sink deeper into. And perhaps love is something that dreams us into being and takes us on life's adventure, rather than something that we can control, "get right", or force into the shape we think it should have.

Finally, the narrative of more has infiltrated every square inch of our lives-with-love, constantly encouraging overperformance. The clue is in the idea of love equalling gains of some kind; material gains, status gains, likes, attention, proof points. There is a market to find love, and a market to demonstrate love, and very many times the real reciprocity, softness, generosity, and celebration that infuses love relationships gets subsumed under the weight of some kind of commodity that supposedly proves love. Is the love as valid if the engagement ring is modest or there is no ring at all? Does the love run more shallow if the birthday card is hand-scribbled? Is a partnership or a parent–child relationship successful if the Instagram sizzle-reel isn't hitting the algorithm?

Love is a song of the soul and the thing we'd go to the end of the earth for, but not because someone is watching us perform it well.

If you can glimpse little pieces of yourself in these stories and examples, take heart in the fact that your way back to yourself is usually in letting go – surrendering all the expectation and effort you are dragging around and discovering what your "natural" actually looks and feels like. Think of it as growing the roots of your love relationships downwards instead of reaching their branches upwards; honesty and presence are key, and we will walk through this together in later chapters.

The Way We Look

As we saw in Chapter 2, the impression we make on other people is a powerful psychological driver that can readily turn into a part of how we think we need to perform to be accepted. Sometimes our motivation is to match the private image we have of ourselves in our mind's eye, and sometimes it is done to match the expectations and preferences of other people. Either one of these motivations is tied to feeling not quite good enough in our natural state, and either one of these motivations can lead to overperformance.

Perhaps the most obvious manifestation of this is through our efforts to change our physical selves to meet culturally implied standards of wellness, fitness, or beauty.

These bodies of ours are alive with intelligence and instinct, landscapes of lived experience.

These faces of ours are etched with our ancestry, expressions of the force of character coursing through our veins and waiting behind the eyes. And yet, so often, we look down on bodies and faces as insufficiencies. We look at them as things that need fixing, even when they are utterly unbroken. This is culturally imbibed in so many of us in the West especially.

I am a yogi and part of a yoga community, practising regularly. It's where I come home to myself, on my mat. It's also where I notice. And I notice that the one-star reviewer in my mind often has some shade to throw about my wrinkly knees or the fact that things just don't stay where they were when I am upside down anymore. The lightning-quick critique might be equally quickly banished on most days, but it has never truly left. Like yoga, it's a practice; something to regenerate. To respect and admire the brilliance of the body as it is, is an act of resistance against a culture of more that would have you believe that to leave something "unfixed" or "exposed" is somehow shameful.

The energetic tones of much of the wellness, fitness, and beauty industry today are those of envy and comparison. Professor Martha Nussbaum describes envy as a painful emotion that focuses us on the advantages of the other and inevitably compares our own situation unfavourably to theirs.[28] Envy involves you feeling a bit hostile, like there is an unspoken, hidden rivalry that leads to chronic tension and a want-to-be-better-than mindset. It's a waste product of a strained ego and a constant focus on yourself. We do think about ourselves a lot! Envy drives a continuous fantasy about what you do not have and what you should get, and it is a recipe for budding self-hatred and resentment of others. What gets sold to you through the industries that seek to make you "look better" is positive emulation – "You could be as awesome as this too" – and emulation has hope and example within it. But that's not the message that calcifies in your mind when you are bombarded incessantly with messages, because in order to be powerful enough to make you buy, those messages also have a subtext that says you ought to be dissatisfied, insecure, even humiliated by "imperfections", and you need "what they have" to change it. There is nothing nourishing in seeking out imperfections to fix. As Buddhist philosopher Thich Nhat Hanh put it, "We should learn to ask 'What's not wrong?' and be in touch with that."[29]

These three places where overperformance shows up clearly – work, love, and how you look – are so central in contemporary life that it is likely that you (all of us) will recognise them. There is one other, perhaps less direct way that we overperform that I want to shine a torch on before we move on and see if you recognise that too – and that is the way that the fear of missing out (FOMO) can get in the way of regeneration and rest.

FOMO

A tried-and-tested driver for overperformance is FOMO. The underbelly of FOMO is the belief that you could be doing more to improve, optimise, expand, or experience life. Even though a person with FOMO often appears as simply exuberant, productive, and willing to suck the last drop out of the day in a way that we might admire, there is very often a little side order of scarcity that goes alongside that ability to cram it all in, and FOMO is actually smack bang in the middle of those overperformance narratives that so many of us swim around in.

FOMO is also characterised by apprehension, emotional angst, and compulsion. It has the energy of forcing things. Sometimes it's low level (squeezing in that one extra commitment at the weekend) and doesn't cause much more than a nagging sensation, and sometimes it's more insistent and causes real mental strain – like the "one-shot" performance mentality we spoke about in Chapter 2 ("What if I don't take this chance and it was the last chance?", "What if I don't make the effort and then – horror – I don't reach my potential? Or my kids don't?", "What if my choosing less results in me *being* less?").

I recall the wave of public excitement in 2024 as the aurora borealis became visible across parts of England that don't normally witness it. I didn't recognise the low-level FOMO at first, until the day after a particularly spectacular sky show where thousands of people competed on social media to demonstrate the brilliance of their personal experience, their optimal vantage point. It was the ultimate selfie; "I was there". I started to wonder how much of that was really FOMO and the desire to be seen to have seen it, to be seen as part of the awe, rather than really feeling the awe. Can we be taken outside of ourselves by cosmic collisions of light if we are jostling for the best shot? Or is there also room in there for a quiet moment with the invisible embrace of that kind of sheer beauty?

It's the same kind of curiosity I feel watching some people dressed to the nines, full of expectation and quiet anxiety on New Year's Eve, waiting, wanting something real to pierce the performance, but unwilling to skip the celebration in case they miss out. I can almost hear their hearts whispering, "Make room for me."

We have more choices than we like to believe sometimes, even if we don't activate them. Those of you who do get FOMO, I'm curious – is your life really a volume proposition where more means best? Do you feel better when you cram more in to avoid missing out, or when you really choose, from real thought and feeling, what you'd like to do with your precious time? And what do you trade in yourself for not missing anything?

Doing less or skipping opportunities can feel loaded with the possibility of disappointing people or letting someone down – as well as the risk of looking like we weren't part of something with high social value – and so we stretch, we don't let opportunity pass us by in any form, and then we find emptiness in our busyness. With FOMO, future thinking takes up all the space where connection to the moment might be.

What all of these examples show us is that overperformance is a snare. It is a type of psychological over-reach that drives us on, constantly in pursuit of ever more. And it's a trap we lower ourselves into, unwittingly but willingly, to the point of desensitisation. To the point of losing ourselves.

Whether you recognise examples of your own overperformance in your work life, your love relationships, how you feel you need to look, with a touch of FOMO here and there, or whether you have devised a whole other list while reading not mentioned here, the essential insight is that where you recognise overperformance is where you have disconnected from your natural self.

What you might notice about your own overperformance offers a set of clues and cues about where you have drifted, and where you have attached yourself more to an industrial mindset – the prioritisation of efficiency, betterment, standardisation, comparison, and gain.

In the next chapter, we're going to take a look at what can and does happen if we ignore those clues and cues, and how you can start to respond if you find yourself at such a threshold. Beyond that, we turn the corner to a better set of possibilities.

5.

CRASHING AND BURNING

It is actually amazing how much we can and will tolerate before the gap between how we think we should be and our reality gets too wide for us to continue faking, repressing, and keeping up a facade, and the choice to stop is removed – by crashing and burning.

I want to say from the outset here that crashing and burning is absolutely not an inevitable outcome of overperforming in certain areas of your life, but I am going to share with you how it can look and how you might approach it if it does happen, not least as a reflective moment for you to recognise how to steer clear of it if you do see it on the horizon. And if you are in the midst of it, my hope is that this chapter helps you to steer through without feeling alone.

Meet Craig:

> *Throughout my work life, I chose more and more pressure. I traded being a BBC news executive, with endless daily deadlines, for being the Director of Politics and Communications at No. 10 Downing Street. Don't get me wrong, it was a major privilege and learning experience, but the performance screw kept turning, down and down.*

Work felt like the end of a boxing match, where you are completely smashed to pieces, beaten up, and you have to pick yourself up again and keep going. On repeat. I ask myself where did such a damaging approach to how I worked come from? Trauma, I guess. I did have a mother who had a personality disorder and a father who didn't really know how to cope with it and just kept going and avoiding the hard stuff. At some point, I decided I didn't want any of that, so I built a mental tunnel out of there as a kid. I decided I would need to build my own future and that it was going to require huge amounts of energy, battling, and effort. It felt like my means of survival.

There was also this idea deep in my psyche that I needed to make a mark on the world. I needed it to have been worthwhile before I died. That need drove many of my behaviours as a TV news editor. I could never accept less; I had to interrogate and improve at all times.

I think I saw it like a deal: that if I worked hard enough, there would be a point where I'd cross a line, and my life would fall into place and I would feel successful and fulfilled. I took it to mean that I should pour all of my attention and energy into work, letting it take precedence over everything else – family, well-being, friendships.

Even when I did crash, I tried to keep it private initially. Looking back, I don't know how I did it. I wasn't sleeping, I was ruminating hugely and constantly anxious, I felt sick. But I was still delivering results and I honestly don't think anyone even noticed in my professional life. I thought of it as inconvenient and I kept the mask on right up to the point that it was clear that I wasn't able to keep delivering in any part of my life anymore really, and I could see that it wasn't going to be just the force of my own will that decided if I was crashing or not.

The thought of changing things was completely alien to me. The solution seemed to be multi-tasking, rising earlier, sleeping less – giving more of me.

I can see now that it was workaholism, a socially acceptable addiction that gave me repeat, fleeting hits of feeling OK before I went back to the anxiety and the pain. And, like many addictions, it was catalysed in trauma and reinforced by non-existent boundaries. All my feelings of self-worth were tied up in achievement, and filling all my hours was a way to block things out, a way to avoid just being there with myself. I guess the bottom line is that I realise that work won't ever love you back. And if you let it, it will suck you dry.

In Craig's story, we can see that burnout doesn't happen overnight. It is a process, a long descent of ignoring and straining and overriding. It is a phenomenon compounded over an extended period by the chronic practice of putting energy into things or to people who drain you and keep you performing versions of yourself that are not quite true or whole; it is not a single event. When it comes, it's been coming for a while. And you saw it coming too; at least, you saw glimpses, you had clues.

There was a sentence that tipped me over into the full-blown symptoms of my own burnout, although I had been teetering on the edge for a while: "We're going to have to have an airlock around this team to get this done."

An airlock. A sealed, pressurised capsule preventing infiltration of air from the external environment. A way to stay 100 per cent sealed into the work and on task, without being flooded by the rest of life, distracted by the air of our generalised humanity.

First, I felt dizzy. *Maybe I'm dehydrated; I've been in this meeting for hours.* Then my heart started racing to the point I felt alarmed. *Oh my God, am I actually having a heart attack? An actual, real heart attack?* I slowed my breathing. My legs felt weak. My head was too hot. I felt "melty" and unable to control what was happening. "Guys, I don't feel right. I'm sorry but I'm going to have to leave." Someone brought me a glass of water.

A colleague took me home, full of compassion. I was silent, completely overwhelmed. What had just happened to me? It was completely beyond my grasp. I opened my apartment door, greeted my dogs, got into bed, and wept.

I stayed there for days. Like an empty husk. There was a vacuum where all my reason normally lived and I couldn't hang on to a single thought. I looked at my reflection in the mirror and felt nothing, vapid. I remained shaky and weak. I slept during the day and watched foxes skulking around the edge of the park between 2am and 5am every night. I could not explain to anyone with any real conviction what was going on in terms that I thought would seem valid or logical. My GP checked all the biology, asked me if I was suicidal, and then told me to take vitamins and a holiday.

Over weeks, I mustered the will to go and immerse myself in deep, cold water. Swim for 10 minutes. Turn my face into the blackness and let go. I walked. Looked at the canopy or the horizon. Noticed without judgement the bucolic details of late-summer landscapes and cracks in pavements, the coral pink of someone's running shoes passing me, a dog with dreadlocks. A sword fight between wasps.

Family were coming to stay. I was so flat, paper thin, in a soul-drought. I couldn't rise and my dullness was palpable. People tried to help, wearing worried frowns, feeling a little agitated or uneasy that I was so "off" and not knowing how to fix it. Work were generous, gave me space. "This is dragging on too long," I thought, naively...

And drag on it did. It was probably a year before I felt like myself again.

Why Burnout Happens

I see burnout as a really uncomfortable process of involuntary transition away from what is no longer working for you. It is particularly likely to happen when we can partly see the issues, talk about the issues, but we don't or can't seem to change anything. As if our body and mind (perhaps we should say body-mind, given we now know just how connected and undivided these things are) is saying, "Hey look here, we've been flashing up the warning signs and giving you the intel for a while now, so like it or not, you're handing over the keys."

Burnout comes when your practices and behaviour in life no longer have a sustainable vision and you don't really know what ideal you are putting daily into practice or what values you are bringing to life in your efforts anymore. You are just ... doing the work. Just moving, and you're not sure where or why you are going. You have lost the ideal that started you there.

For me, this happened when I found myself around an executive table talking about scaling up and expansion and financial profit and loss, and no longer working intimately as a psychologist, with people. For you, it might be the amount of time you put into curriculum admin instead of teaching, or into reporting instead of nursing. An early-career graduate I know is already questioning the ideals that got him into the world of consumer financial protection as he navigates hugely shifting politics in the USA. The values and ideals that motivate your work matter enormously, and we will explore this some more in Chapter 7.

Or it might be that you do have a vision, secret or spoken, and that vision cannot find a way to reach into your life properly. Perhaps because you can't find a gap in between the churn of daily life to turn your ideas into intentions, your intentions into decisions, and your decisions into practices, or because you're avoiding yourself and what you stand to lose, or gain. Maybe your ideal was to work for yourself and you know that you are capable, but you never took the step in case it didn't work, so you're still grinding away at the job you find dull. You still feel anxious that you should make a move, but the idea of it feels weaker and weaker each time it comes up, like an insect trying earnestly to escape through a window by repeatedly hitting the glass, until it fades and you feel out of energy.

When the gap between what you desire and your reality gets too wide, generally something has to give. That "give" might be leaving a job or a chronically troubled relationship, finally saying no to the ever-growing set of obligations that you have slid sideways into without ever really agreeing (but never really disagreeing either), or weaving some boundaries around what it is that you need and want before your energy bleeds out into all the performances that you do, but don't really want to do. If we don't voluntarily "give", we involuntarily "give".

We don't burn out *just* because we do a lot; we burnout because what we do fails to give meaning to our lives or renew our imaginations, our senses and sensuality, and our feeling of being in integrity with the things our hearts know matter the most.

Sacrificing, investing, building, creating – indeed the hard graft of performing – all matter. I don't wish to diminish any of these noble and valid efforts or cares, but I do wish to turn your attention to whether (a) that hard graft, investing, building, and so on, is creating something that is true, harmonious, and whole for you, a web of real relationships that arouse love or care in you, and a life that you yourself find beautiful and (b) you are still connected to yourself and in balance while you perform, or whether you are numbed out and ignoring yourself while you push beyond your limits.

For Merlin, who we first met in Chapter 2, burnout came from the strain of that huge gap between how he felt in his heart and what he thought he should feel based on his cultural narratives and personal mentalities:

> *I look back now after some serious time out to heal and I could weep at how willing I was to sacrifice myself on the*

altar of other people's perceptions. For the longest time, I ignored my heart and I couldn't face myself. I wanted a different life, one that was probably much less impressive but much more honest, for me. I didn't know how to think about it other than to believe that the problem was with me, some kind of lack that I couldn't accept because it didn't fit with my values. But I never felt right, or "whole". I denied my truth for years and could not change course, and I completely went up in flames because of it. My body was the only part of me that could tell the truth by crashing and burning. I nearly lost myself, on many levels.

Understanding What Is Happening

When something is awry and we are on a mission to fix it, we really love a label. It offers a surface-level understanding and sense of control in the face of complexity and stress, and often, thankfully, a remedial pathway forward.

Something like burnout, though, is very hard to pin down and therefore easy to brush over. The term itself has contested origins, but the story that appeals to me most in terms of the vivid image it evokes is from the 1970s, where it was borrowed from heroin and other narcotic users who had injected into their over-punctured veins so often that they could no longer inject without a searing burning sensation that overwhelmed the pleasure of the drug itself. They might keep trying, chasing, but the pain-free return was never there again. That feels true for burnout too – you cannot keep pushing when you're "punctured"; it's time for repair. I also like the image of a burnt-out building with the facade intact but a void inside that a passer-by might never notice. People who are burning out or burnt out often hide it, either because they feel shame at not being able to carry on, because it doesn't make any sense and doesn't fit with their self-view, or they imagine that it will quickly pass – "Just a tough moment, I've had plenty of those before, push on." But the overperformance that leads to burnout is not just a tough moment, it is chronic and it is insidious, taking over who you are and how you act without you realising it.

In his book, *What Nobody Tells You About Burnout*, researcher and author Marcos Mendanha describes the trickiness of the term burnout, saying it is an overly used, overly broad, generic, and tangled term, sometimes a condition itself, sometimes a syndrome, sometimes a vague and ill-defined exhaustion.[30] You have probably heard the term used casually this week, in the same way we use the term "depressed" when we are slightly disappointed that there isn't a new season of *Ted Lasso* yet.

Something gets called a "syndrome" when it shows a stable and constant set of symptoms, but its causes are not yet fully understood scientifically; once it is, well, then we call it a "disease". But those experiences where body, mind, and (don't say it out loud) soul are entangled, rather than in separate boxes that get separate labels and separate treatment, can be harder to understand. This is really tough when we have such a preference to remove doubt.

But even a clinical diagnosis doesn't account for the soul-sickness you feel, or won't account for the cultural malaise that is part of the burden of burnout. It cannot account for the colour washing out of life, or the unnerving, disembodied, and fragmented feeling of no longer knowing what to do next, because clinical diagnosis, by definition, is about reduction to a clear cause and effect, and burnout is, if anything, messy. To me, the loss of compass that a person experiences is what makes burnout a soul-event; something that might take you to dark places, but that can also create depth, maturing, or ripening of your identity.

Burnout has a huge diversity and breadth of symptoms and there is no single, timeless, unified, or predictable experience of it. What you might experience can include feelings of physical fatigue and depletion, low immunity and repeatedly getting sick, or not able to shake things off quickly.

You might be burdened with insomnia, headaches, shortness of breath for no reason, loss of appetite, low sex drive, gastrointestinal issues, and heaviness in your body.

You might experience cognitive "fog", which is like an inability to think clearly for very long, and when you *are* thinking, you might not be able to fish out that one clear understanding or idea or sentence that would normally be right there for you.

As part of burnout's mental exhaustion, you might experience a loss of motivation, a lack of passion, boredom, indifference, big feelings of disillusionment (even if you can't nail down why), even numbness – a real reduction in your overall mojo, so to speak.

You might also have deep feelings of disappointment with yourself and with others, feeling cynical, defensive, and angry, be startlingly quick to tears, and very much at the whim of mood swings. Or maybe you find yourself being more rigid, impatient, or stubborn than usual. Burnout can put your normal mental and emotional resilience on the floor.

Maybe the slow descent into burnout has made you feel paranoid, full of self-doubt, confused, or even guilty about not feeling what you "should" feel or wanting what you "should" want and worrying that other people will know and judge you for it.

For many of us, burnout brings an impoverishment of meaning and kind of dries out the inner and outer life. It's awful.

To cope, some people turn to excessive numbing behaviours like substance use, gambling, shopping, even more overworking, porn, doomscrolling, overeating, overstimulating, and overconsuming in all sorts of ways, and this further confuses the process of diagnosing, especially where burnout may overlap with many other mental illness diagnostic categories like depression or addiction, and where behaviours like these can propel people into burnout in the first place.

This entanglement of experiences, plus burnout seeming to rebel against being categorised, means that treatment for burnout can't be standardised or even claimed as effective in traditional Western medical terms. In the absence of both label and standardised treatment, burnout often gets referenced instead as an occupational problem or perhaps a personal psychological issue – mental suffering and pain, sure, but maybe not a "real" medical issue. This is taxing for every person suffering from burnout who is already confused or masking their symptoms.

In addition, as we explored in the last chapter, the kind of overperformance that can lead to burnout is definitely not just an occupational issue. It can happen in marriages, in friendships, in parenting, or any area of your life that you invest in, in such a way that you abandon yourself in order to keep pushing forward and performing.

To me, if burnout is *like* anything, it is more *like* grief – "a living loss", as psychotherapist Julia Samuel says;[31] a painful, disorienting *process* of involuntary loss and letting go. As is so often the case with other forms of grief, we'd rather leave it outside with the door firmly closed on this unwelcome guest. But I think we can use burnout, if it arrives, as an opening to deeper wholebeing, as we are going to explore.

Extraordinary numbers of people are experiencing something like this phenomenon of chronic, unmanaged stress, exhaustion, and depletion. The experience that you are personally having – that sense of independently "losing it" or being unwell – is not independent at all.

You are not alone in your experience, but in good and broad company, because many people feel, even if they can't explain it, that they have outgrown those versions of performance that burn them out but are melted into their skulls as good and necessary. This is not your problem, really. It is a collective social problem that we all need to address.

You could say that burnout shape-shifts and mimics our cultural lives; we continue to be separate and isolated from each other and the web of life; we continue to think that good enough means exceptional and superior to others; we continue to think that we need to get more efficient and more accomplished at all times in all ways; and we continue to see life through the lens of what more we want and need to have for ourselves in order to have "arrived" at success or happiness. If burnout happens to you – which again, is not inevitable – you might find yourself trying to deal with it privately, in isolation, and in control – like Craig in the story shared earlier. It is really tough to digest what is happening just from within your own mind; this is something for us to do communally. Burnout and its recovery is a time to turn to community and friendship for help metabolising such a big emotional and physical shift. It's a time to be held, to keep warm.

When we don't stop and do the work to heal

It's not so easy to stop and face the truth of yourself if you are chronically overperforming somewhere in your life and causing yourself to suffer. But we fan the flames of burnout when we live in denial and never allow ourselves to rest in what's true today, however uncomfortable it is.

It's so tempting to deny what is failing, to resist the fact that some aspect of what we are doing has just run out of steam, didn't work, needed different skills, or didn't last. Maybe you kind of know that you really need to pivot, reinvent, reimagine, or move on in order to reclaim that sense of possibility within you, but it's overwhelming. It might feel easier for you to stay with the way things are today, even if you are hanging on by your fingernails, because the insecurity that goes with change feels too much. Even the freedom that comes with endings can feel too much – too unknown and exposed – and it seems easier to bury your desire to end something than to face the reality and volatility of change.

I get it. It's tough stuff. Sometimes, we find that we don't really love what we thought we loved. Sometimes, we no longer want what it was that we chased so hard for.

Likewise, it is tempting to deny our fears, pretending it's all good because we'd rather avoid what might happen if we say our truth out loud and disappoint people, anger people, get cancelled, rock the boat, look weird, get rejected, make a bad move, or lose traction.

But denial of our feelings is costly to our wholebeing. Pretending that we're not drained, bored, depleted, strained, unhappy, or disinterested can become *utterly normal* if we let it.

Denying fear doesn't make it go away, it allows it to resurface in sketchy ways and ambushes us or projects out on to other people.

Build-up and denial

If you recognise yourself in these descriptions, it's probable that you haven't ostensibly just kept your head in the sand until you crashed. More likely, your awareness of both yourself and the situation you found yourself in waxed and waned, sometimes solid and illuminated, perhaps in a moment of crisis, sometimes fleeting and vague, business as usual.

You might have noted "the gap" in your authenticity here and there, but not really believed it or wanted to believe it – looking away from the direction that your heart was calling for and towards the direction that your mind was insisting was necessary.

You might have known that something had to give, or something needed attention or healing, but not acted. When we do this, we avoid emotionally metabolising what is going on in our lives or, we could say, we avoid repairing the ruptures that occur.

Our lives are full of "ruptures" – disturbances or breaches or cracks that happen in the course of normal living, especially in our close relationships. Psychologist John Gottman suggested that it is not the fact that we fight that is the problem, but it is the way that fights are handled, and conflict of all types do not come out of the blue, but are part of a repeating cycle of rupture and repair.[32]

I believe this cycle of rupture and repair also applies to our relationship to work and our relationship to community, culture, and the broader web of life. Ruptures are inevitable, part of the cycle of intimacy, understanding, and belonging – maybe they are even necessary for continual expansion and evolution – but if we keep taking the ruptures and ignoring the repairs, we become eroded.

Emotional ruptures are the ones that need the most time in the "repair shop" of our hearts. Perhaps you see yourself, on the whole, as very capable and pragmatic at dealing with practical, personal ruptures in life, however painful – things that go wrong or were not planned and cause disruption and drama. You've made it this far after all! Perhaps you are also most likely to ask for help from other people on the practical stuff. It's the emotion that runs parallel to practical ruptures that stings. It's not the material uncertainty of leaving a job, it's the feeling of shame or failure that goes with it, even if the choice is solid. It's not the disruption of a break-up and changing the circumstances of your life, it's the ricochet from the meanness or ugly behaviour between people, and the grief that goes with it. It's not the disruption and life change that comes with serious ill health, it's the fear that goes with it.

Add to that the emotional ruptures that feel so big and amorphous that we simply have no idea how to repair or heal them. For example, knowing that the kind of future a 10-year-old will have will not be recognisable to us and we don't confidently know how to give hope or protect or guide; or the angst and anger about whether the geopolitical instability across the world will turn to world war, or how to acknowledge and face the violence in current wars; or whether the changes in our climate will hit tipping points that are irrevocable. There is no way that the repeated positioning of existential crises for humanity on the news each night does not create emotional rupture and fear for us. We are truly not inside a bubble. These ruptures all smoulder in us and need our response at some level, and we know it in our bones.

Maybe we have a moment where the force of truth that we feel wrung out erupts in our lives – perhaps catalysed by a disagreement, a loss, or some other moment of deep vulnerability, and we have a beam of clarity like a ray of sunlight rippling down from a crack in the clouds. "This is not OK. I have to act."

What does "I have to act" look like, you may ask. Does it have to be gigantic acts? Conspicuous acts? Do I have to … change? Or can the act be more like a tiny little nudge? Compound small acts can, of course, be useful – it's how we build habits and practices – but take care that small acts are indeed steps towards what is really true for you and not steps away from what you want to avoid. And all acts, big and small, must come from feeling as well as thought; from the heart as well as the mind.

Your small nudges may relieve some pain, but as Vanessa Machado De Oliveira says, pain relief is not pain release.[33] Small nudges are not the same as rupture repairs. In fact, temporary pain relief sometimes acts more like repression or denial. When you are on the road to burnout, whatever it is that put you here does have to *change*. Pausing or plastering over the cracks does nothing to soothe the transition – the real moving through.

Here's the bottom line, lovely people: you cannot repair, heal, or move towards wholebeing until you transition away from what is not working for you today. You need to uproot the old before you can replant the new; deconstruct your old ways before you can reconstruct some new ones. And sometimes, getting beyond your current state of un-health might require real disruption. You are already walking that path of release by being here, still reading and reflecting – perhaps further down it than you think – and you have resources within and without that we are going to illuminate. Instead of keeping that unwelcome guest of pain or grief or fear outside a tightly closed door, in doing this work you are choosing something different – maybe we could even consider it to be a kind of hospitality, an open door and willingness to listen to ourselves once again.

After burnout, I had to trace my being-ness back down to the root – a word that shares its origins with the word "radical"; the root of why I was moving so fast and forcefully and the radical solution it provided me at that time: keep moving, don't get stuck, hold all the weight, eyes on the horizon, suck it up. Often it has "worked" for me in terms of outputs and outcomes and long lists of achievements, but never in terms of wholeness. It never served love.

"What's at the root of your overperformance and what radical solution did it serve for you?" is a question that doesn't get answered intellectually, but by the heart. And there, in all the sloppy emotional mud, is where I recognised myself and all my compromises, my fragments. I recognised the wax and wane of my courage to be still and surrender to the experience I was having, like that water nymph drying out on the reed, waiting to fully open up and see things anew.

Burnout forced me to replay and watch all the ways I am swimming in the cultural narratives of separateness, exceptionalism, endless optimisation, and needing more. There was no energy to push through and distract myself from their truths, or from the truth of my own remaining, untended pain.

Burning out, as awful as it is, is a big, uncomfortable disturbance that offers us that chance to transition. As the poet Robert Frost said, "the best way out is always through".[34]

A Way Through

When it comes to burnout and a way through it, as always, I find a natural wisdom in ecology – in this case, the ecology of wildfire.

Wildfire is something most of us fear because of the obvious loss and devastation it can bring, especially as the planet warms, the population spreads, and age-old fire-management practices change. Wildfire presents real danger, and never more so than when natural wildfire is repressed for too long and the blaze is extreme and savage.

Us humans like to think we can keep everything steady and that everything can and should be controlled, and that when something "bad" does happen, it's a freak of nature, a problem to be fixed. Nature shows us a different way.

I wonder what we might learn about ourselves and our own internal "fire-management practices" and "post-burn" regeneration approach that could be useful?

Ecological systems, like coniferous forests, savannahs, grasslands, steppes, prairies, and eucalyptus forests, have evolved with fire as an essential contributor to a healthy habitat. Fire is seen as necessary and, in some ways, valuable, albeit consequential and full of danger.

Wildfire is not always a good thing by any stretch, but sometimes good things can be generated from the ashes.

For example, many plant species in fire-affected environments use fire to germinate their seeds, to reproduce, or to establish themselves for the first time in the space. These are known as fugitive and pioneer species, and they cannot actually come to life without either smoke or fire in their environment. They may lay dormant for years, like the South African fire lily, waiting for heat to stimulate it into new life and reclaim its colour and presence in the landscape. I wonder what seeds of your own fugitive ideas could be sitting under the dry soil in your life, waiting for the lick of a flame to bring out your colour? I wonder what pioneering narratives and stories about the life you'd like to create are there, waiting for an opportunity to be explored, a bit of light on them to get going?

Wildfire is also seen as an integral part of maintaining biodiversity in some environments, and some organisms within these fire-affected communities have even adapted to withstand and exploit natural fires, something known as a biotic response. Many of the clients I have worked with during and post-burnout have found their own biotic response, like a storyteller just getting into the garden and slowly creating with it until her own creative ideas came back into bud after being in a "mono-cropped" work environment for too long, or a paramedic starting a successful platform to connect and support disillusioned frontline workers after burning out himself.

Indeed, the suppression of natural fires in forests and on grasslands – fires that need to happen – can really reduce diversity. Could denying or avoiding "the heat" we feel brewing in our own lives be contributing to feeling stuck and stale? Are we building up too much "combustible material" (resentment, fatigue, boredom, stress) that might make a burnout really extreme later? Is overperforming at one thing costing us diversity in life? Denying the opportunity for new, different growth patterns?

Wildfires have many components that offer us rich metaphors for considering burnout.

Consider the severity and impact of the fire. Some wildfires are low impact and might not make a visible or material difference to the environment. Likewise, burnout in humans can happen across a continuum of intensity, with some people feeling singed or scorched by their symptoms, but still able to function, and others feeling like charcoal. There is no one pattern or set of symptoms that validates your own "psychological wildfire".

Ground fires burn through soil that is rich in organic matter, what is known as "the understory". What is the story under your own burnout, I wonder? What beliefs, ideas, myths, narratives in that fizzing soil are ready to catch on fire? The idea of never being enough or safe enough? The myth of urgency? The narrative in the back of your mind that says that you are different to everyone else you have seen this happen to, and it wouldn't happen to you?

Surface fires burn through the understory like ground fires, but also through living and dead plant material close to the ground. A surface fire might leave the tall timbers intact and even leave a forest looking relatively unscathed, but it burns ground-level fuels and takes out the rich diversity of life closer to the roots. This reminds me again of Craig's story – of ignoring all the diverse parts of his life, like family, friendships, and health, so that he could focus entirely on work, and then, when the tall timber fell, there was nothing left to hold the ecosystem together.

And then there are crown fires that burn through the tops of shrubs and trees, at times making huge leaps between the canopies and creating a rapid spread.

Sometimes, deadwood that is still standing and hasn't yet rotted to the forest floor can create what is called a fuel ladder, spreading surface fires to the canopy. Likewise, those emotions, tensions, and traumas that we don't address and allow to compost as we go, can create a bigger psychological "fuel ladder" when burnout comes.

Crown fires are also considered the most dangerous, the most overwhelming and hardest to control, and are often fuelled by strong winds – weather and climate conditions beyond our immediate control. Those climatic and cultural "winds" in human life, like pandemics and wars and climate change and the unknown future of living with AI, most certainly add energy to the wildfires in our psychology. Some days, it feels like it is only gravity holding us up among the overwhelm. As Jon Kabat-Zinn said, overwhelm is the feeling that "our lives are somehow unfolding faster than the human nervous system and psyche are able to manage well".[35] It seems to me that this is a very good reason to manage both the surface (our behaviours) and the understory (our narratives and mentalities).

It is true that wildfires can start from a random lightning strike, but, more often, the risk comes during an extended dry period where there is low airflow and not enough hydration, and when the ground work has not been done. This is the same for burnout. If we don't have "psychological firebreaks", the risk of burnout continues.

There is an alternative, and the rest of this book is dedicated to helping you find it.

This change starts with letting go.

PART 3.

CROSSING THRESHOLDS

So far in this book, we have built a picture of how so many people get to strain, suffering, and potential burnout through overperformance. Seeing your own picture come into focus is hard, admirable work. Take a moment to acknowledge yourself for that. From here, the goal is to deconstruct that picture and reconstruct one that helps you travel in a different direction.

The deconstruction – especially the part that requires real honesty – isn't always easy on the ego. That can be extra spicy at those times when we feel worn out, so if you are worn out, remember the ASAP acronym, as seen through a regenerative performance lens: as slow as possible, as soft as possible, as sincere as possible, as soulful as possible. It's also worth remembering through this section that overperformance almost always stems from the good intention to get things right – you aren't doing things all wrong if you are an overperformer, you might just have more beneficial, positive, and strengthening options in front of you.

At the same time, you might start to recognise yourself again, start to get glimpses of what it is like to feel at home in your own life and calm in your inner space, which can be a relief. Coming home to yourself is, in essence, starting to think and feel through your wholebeing. Staying whole does not require you to know all of the answers – in fact, the uncertainty can be fertile ground for trying something different. It begins from a felt state, the sensing of "home" inside of yourself that sets the tone for telling your truth and getting aligned.

These next two chapters are all about supporting you to do that.

6.

COMING HOME

If you find yourself exhausted and stressed out from years of overperforming, I'm glad you are here, at the point of change. Maybe you are on the cusp of burning out and ready to make a shift and regain your feet, or perhaps you have already crossed that breach. Maybe you are simply interested in reimagining what a life with more aliveness and vitality might look like, and the overperformance picture you have been building is helping you to see where you could tidy up here and there, and find some new ways of expanding and regenerating your energy. Either way, now is a good time for radical (to the root) self-care, psychological hygiene, and a genuine willingness to adjust beyond doing the same things that got you here. The poet Rumi said: "Sit, be still, and listen, for you are drunk, and we're at the edge of the roof." It's solid advice.[36]

I know it can certainly feel overwhelming to think about how much effort you have put in and put out through your life and then find yourself unsure, uneasy, and *really* tired. That is not wasted effort. Nothing is ever wasted. Nothing is ever lost if you can see that an ending will also become a beginning – an opportunity to reclaim more of yourself that matters and to navigate differently. In truth, we can't stockpile progress, performances, or achievements and assume they are a guarantee of a well and happy life, an endless upwards track. In the last chapter, I used the metaphor of wildfires to describe how things build and break down, sometimes for the greater good. Everything in nature is part of a cycle, and that includes the breaking down of what no longer serves, what no longer has life in it. You can't go back to what was if you want to thrive – that's not how evolution works. Softening and surrendering what has finished is necessary, even if you don't want to let go. Even burning up can be part of the cycle. It all feeds what is to come.

A tremendously important framing that I want to offer here if you are burnt out or on the cusp of it, or simply feeling that how you are living and working isn't quite right, is that this is no time for self-judgement about how you have failed, because this is lostness, not failure. It's why I titled this chapter "Coming Home"; coming back to a feeling of rightness and naturalness within you and within the world around you, and leaving the tight pretence and exhausting overperformance behind. What is needed is what Adrienne Maree Brown has called a "loving correction";[37] an accountability to self and other that comes from understanding where the harm is coming from, and what it is that you can do to let it go. Coming home means acknowledging where you are at, really, and trying to turn down the volume of your own criticism while you do so.

When we hit a roadblock and run out of steam, we often seek to put ourselves back together enough to resume what we were doing and "get back to it". We are conditioned to start with action, something new, better, brighter than this – a resolution, a challenge, a new job, a reboot, a big holiday from the bucket list, or something else that can be ticked off in order to feel like things are back on track. Can you see the same patterning? The same lack of acceptance of the whole you rather than just the performer? The resistance to being right here, without feeling the need to climb or improve yourself?

Every time you move to action when you are exhausted, you smother the parts of you that are suffering. You ignore the spiritual weariness, the physical depletion, the plain old mental tiredness. A "lift" of action, of course, gives you quick feedback – "Yes, we're on the move, get me outta here." Action offers you a ready place to channel your angst and feel a productive energy. But it is not always what's needed. It is more of the same stress-scrambling. That angst is telling you something you need to hear, and stopping to listen works for you, not against you. It is time to be more faithful to yourself. Your truth is not dangerous, but your suppression of it is.

The hardest part of shifting from overperformance to regenerative performance may well be giving permission to yourself not to try to immediately diagnose, fix, and get back in the saddle. Your wellness, your wholeness, cannot be reduced to a label, a list, or made into another thing to quickly improve and manage – especially not with a commercial product, however tempting they are. Tune in to how often those quick-fix product adverts try to convince you to go back to your best or leap forward to a better you. They tell you that the way you are today is wrong, dangerous, and in need of a product. You know these cultural narratives now – they are sneaky and seductive, and they keep you overperforming. That said, therapies of various kinds, from talk therapy, somatic therapy, and plant medicine, to hypnotherapy or EMDR (eye movement desensitisation and reprocessing – a psychotherapy that helps people recover from trauma by reprocessing traumatic memories), for example, can be a great support for some people in the meandering process of "coming home". Regardless, you still have to trust that no one knows you better than you do. The whole point is to reclaim yourself from those cultural mind traps and relentless-pushing habits. But maybe you have forgotten how "you" feels without them.

And so, the number-one task is to come back and recognise your whole and real self, again and again, even if it's just a glimpse at first, starting with getting back to basics.

Back to Basics

Whether you are in the cut and thrust of overperforming and know it's not truly working for you, or you have tipped over into burnout, one of your central experiences will probably be confusion and self-doubt that you may be trying to solve with doubling down and gritting it out – basically ignoring yourself and doing more. That, my friend, is not going to work.

When you are so mentally fatigued that your mind feels like mush, it's time to reclaim the basics. If your head is on fire, and your body doesn't really even feel like it belongs to you, it's time to reconnect. And before you start sifting through your life and mentally assessing what to do next, it is worth – as best as you can manage – coming back to an integrated state of being.

"The basics" in my view are decent sleep, real nourishment, movement, deliberate relaxation, being around people who you don't have to "perform" with, and awakened senses. Many wonderful resources and expert guidance are available to support you to understand the first five areas if you need them.

Senses are not normally considered part of the basics, but I want to encourage you to see yourself as whole, connected to and part of the vast web of life, and not just alive within the skin of your own body. I also want to encourage you to uproot the idea of yourself as a series of machine-like components that need attention (your body, your mind, and so on), and that some kind of routine service or adjustment in each will sort you out – like a diet, a new cardio programme, or a more positive attitude. This is not a moment for a goal-based reset or a challenge. This is about re-establishing a basic harmony within yourself.

When you pay attention to the basics, you can do so with a wider lens than just that of your thinking mind. You can also use your intuition and your own nervous system as guides, and they will often tell you everything you need to know about what you really need. You can also give yourself permission to be imperfect, experimental, curious, or expansive.

The recognised well-being wisdom is that seven to nine hours' sleep per night is healthy. Who doesn't love a great night's sleep? But many overperformers and those who have burnout find sleep to be a fickle frenemy that visits at inconvenient times. And so they wrestle and wriggle through the night, tossing and turning themselves further into frustration, reaching for the smartphone at their bedside a dozen times, turning the pillow to the cold side, and ultimately frowning themselves through a few patchy hours before breakfast caffeine and carbs save them, temporarily.

When you are able to get a hold of these basics, you may find that you have better energy for building new, regenerative habits, and the practices suggested to help you "come home" feel more readily accessible.

Quieten the Mind

You probably know from experience that the pull towards driving yourself and overdoing it is strong – even if it just shows up as a negative critical voice in your head and doesn't make it to action: "You are so lazy; wow, just get on with it" or "You could have at least done…" or "By Tuesday you should have…" or maybe "You have not moved this week so you definitely cannot just sit here and…"

Whether you do the things or restrain yourself from the things on that deliriously long to-do list or not, the judgement that you *should* creates psychological strain. It makes you psychologically busy, not just physically busy.

This is something that is hyper-normal in our culture. When we "over"-do something, we are acting in the extreme, to excess, exaggerating, or doing it to the point of exhaustion. It is also called "going beyond", and you may have literally got an award for it. Overdoing it has become so lauded in our society that it can sometimes feel like the extra mile is the only mile that matters. The 10 per cent that comes after the 100 per cent is the per cent that gets recognised most warmly. Busyness has become a badge of honour and esteem. That drive to overcome, live busy, and push forward is richly entangled in our ideas about being good and good enough, and I suspect that we have lost sight of the fact that going beyond is something that needs to be used sparingly, rarely, and precisely.

Yes, we have another gear. Yes, we can take on more. We can often push way harder than we think we can, and our mindset has a great deal to do with that, but my proposition is that we do not take nearly enough mindful care in deciding, rationally, on where or how to deploy that grit. We expect grit to be a permanent, on-demand feature used everywhere and on everything. It's neither sustainable nor desirable to do that.

There are many simple practices that start the process of pressing pause, breaking the busy spell, and quietening the mind for a moment. Here is an example:

Take a moment to get comfortable where you are, perhaps in a seat that you can lean back into, allowing it to take your weight as you drop your shoulders and stretch out your palms. Notice the place where your feet meet the floor. Notice if you are holding any tension in your face or neck and just release it a bit if so, maybe with some small movements.

When you feel settled, focus your gaze on one small thing and notice it. Carefully and slowly describe it to yourself in as much detail as you can, with no agenda other than to describe what you see. When your mind interferes with some chat, which it will, dismiss it gently and come back to your observations.

The example in front of me as I type this are the woven fabric stripes on my notebook next to me – black, orange, and white. The stripes are different widths and there is about double the amount of black and white stripes to orange. Some of the orange is a little faded where the book has been handled the most. The pages are thick, cream-coloured, and a bit tatty. There is a copper ribbon bookmark sticking out of the bottom left-hand corner (mind adds "you need to get a new notebook, this one is almost done" … ignore). I can see a beam of sunlight pouring in through the window to the left of me and hitting the top of the desk. As I focus on it, I can see all sorts of colours within it, and a lot of dust particles (mind immediately instructs me to add cleaning to my list … ignore).

Allow yourself to mentally browse the small observations over and again, several times. Describe the details to yourself.

Add an audible breath with the back of your throat closed, loud enough that you can hear it and so it sounds a bit like a wave lapping on the shore. Then take another, longer one through your nose and notice where it wants to stop – your throat, your chest? Keep going for a few long, slow breaths, ever so gently – just allow it to flow.

Keep the slow and simple focus on the descriptions of what you chose to look at while you breathe. Keep your gaze soft. Allow your chest to rise and fall with the flow of breath. As you breathe, allow an almost imperceptible rhythm to develop in your describing. Orange stripe, dancing dust…

Do this for about a few minutes, which might feel like five years, then let go. Put your hand across your heart space and notice. Notice your body, those tired shoulders. The balls of your feet, your slightly clenched jaw. Notice whether your tongue is pushed up against the roof of your mouth or resting. Notice the connection between your hand and your chest.

This is You. Do you remember?

When you can let go, even just for a moment, in all of that mental noise about where you are supposed to be, what you are supposed to be doing, and what you should have achieved by now, you might recognise yourself, fleetingly at least. You might also feel a prickle of sadness up into your chest at that recognition, because you spend so little time hanging out with that version of you – that steady-breathing being with so much aliveness coursing through their veins.

You are not just your whirring, fantastical mind, not just a psychological energy contained in a brain. You are a natural being with soul. You are life, here and now. Coming home to yourself is, in a sense, like rewilding your psychology – reconnecting with those aspects of you that have become disconnected from both nature-inside and nature-outside; from your innate wisdom and your body; and from the web of living things you are part of.

Instead of conforming to tight cultural standards and expectations that busyness will be the path to goodness and greatness, problems or threats, how about you reclaim some of your inherent wildness? How about you start to trust your intuitions and instincts, rather than relying on your rational thought to tell you how you are doing? Your psychology is also in your gut and your heart, in your awe and wonder, your curiosity, your senses and sensuality. It is in your response to touch and sound and taste, and especially in your response to being in natural environments. I am not talking about hiking the Pacific Crest Trail, I'm talking about reclaiming your home inside yourself, and your home within the living world. That is rewilding your psychology, and it requires you to unlearn a whole heap of conditioning.

Slow Down

Slowness is a speed that we seem to have forgotten and one that I have come to see as essential to re-familiarise ourselves with. It is not the only pace or even the better pace to live by – I believe that diversity of paces is better for wholebeing and for regenerative performance – but some slowness is certainly needed when we are depleted physically and emotionally.

Over the last few years of my practice, I have been using Slow Coaching with one-on-one clients mostly from the world of high-performance sport and entertainment. Slow Coaching is a kind of retreat work that requires a person to come to a remote place in a natural/wild setting for three days, for deep nourishment and psychological work. It always starts with the senses. It might be halfway through the time we have together before we "work" in a more traditional sense, before a piece of paper is laid on the table or a pen held in hand, which can feel a little uncomfortable for people still attached to the clock. But Slow Coaching is a form of deep feedback and not just an opportunity to unravel some challenges for a person.

Most clients arrive in a state of prolonged stress, often as overperformers. Their cortisol is through the roof and their minds are scanning like search beams, seeking out the path forwards, upwards, to an improved, idealised version of themselves. They have been looking for answers and certainty. They don't recall how to be strategic with their energy or who they want to be around, who supports their energy rather than extracts from it. They have no idea yet what their body intelligence has to contribute. And often they can't clearly recall what it is they love anymore.

We night walk. We hike on moorland. We wild swim or ice bathe and sauna. We cook over fire. We chop wood or plant things. We eat real food full of flavour and depth. We talk. We notice. We breathe. We nourish. It is the polar opposite of quick hits of junk-dopamine and one-line-headline solutions. It is reclamation. After a couple of days, a person can begin to think from wholebeing and not from anxiety. They almost always have their own answer to their problem or challenge part-formed through both thought and intuition, but they just haven't been "home" enough to trust themselves.

It always humbles me to hear, six months later, what moment of insight a client had on a night walk while in awe of an owl swooping and in full possession of their senses despite the lack of visibility. It is amazing and yet not surprising to see a person come to tears in recognition that they have not felt like themselves for so long, even though the world sees a leader and a champion, or to see a person look back at themselves and where they have been askew with a flicker of recognition, once they have created some psychological space. It is dropping into slowness that lets you experience such clarity and space.

Listen to What Is Here

There is no way to just think yourself out of burnout or a stuck place, or out of the web of narratives and behaviours that put you there in the first place. You have to feel too. You have to reconnect and recognise. And to do that, as storyteller Daniel Firth Griffith says, "you have to create the quiet space where the harvest doesn't have to happen".[38]

One way to find such a quiet space is to find something small, seemingly unimportant, and temporary to engage with each day. Make it something organic, not digital – ideally something that you can do with your hands or that involves easy, repetitive movements. I have a client who dug and planted a garden – when she felt she had absolutely no energy for anything cognitive, she could dig holes and put seeds in them. Another person became temporarily obsessed with carving spoons, something that he started to avoid his screaming desire to go and pick up his phone in the other room. Another client fixed his lawnmower that had been broken in the shed for about 1,000 years. Another walked slowly for miles around his city and photographed doorways he'd never noticed before with his "real" camera. I knitted scarves for every unsuspecting person I knew, never actually learning how to knit "properly" but enjoying the rhythmic clicking of needles and the feel of the wool in my hands, and, most importantly, the clean, uncomplicated focus on one thing. It doesn't matter what it is, no need to judge it. It just matters that you are there with it.

In the first few weeks, my client who walked his city with his camera was focused on the architectural details and colour palettes of the doorways, allowing himself to imagine the lives of the people who lived and worked beyond them and, sometimes, comparing that fantasy to the mess he thought his own life was in. He noted that he had an expectation that he'd always take a picture of a different, ever-more-interesting doorway on his walks at first, compiling a little album and comparing which was "best". He judged his walks as "silly", but kept going each day. After a while, and maybe as his nervous system began to settle down with the rest from the massively busy executive role he normally had, he started to notice himself too. I asked him to notice his breath as he moved as a start. Then he noticed the way his feet connected with the pavement and that the left was quite different from the right, and that it actually hurt and he'd forgotten. He noticed how tight his shoulders were as he hunched them right up to his ears while he walked, keeping himself contained and sealed off from the world. As he held his camera up to his face one day, he noticed his own hands, so familiar in one way but also, the new wrinkles, the scar on his wrist, the mark where his wedding band had been, barely within his recognition. "I have seen and done so much with these hands," he said, "and I hardly see them as part of me." His eyes welled up with tears.

He started to notice his senses again, the smell of bread 150 metres away from the bakery on the corner that made him hungry, the cold morning air on his face, two women laughing with the kind of shriek that had "best friend" written all over it. But he also noticed "senses" that were unfamiliar too, other forms of intelligence that he was totally tuned out from before. He noticed when a young woman crossed the street to avoid him on a particularly early walk when the light was pale. He noticed when he felt open to a person's energy as they exchanged hellos, and that it lifted him a little. He noticed that he felt helpless and ashamed when walking past a dishevelled older man on the street. He noticed how much he liked and disliked many of his doorways, depending on whether they invited entry, spoke of a home, or their cold grey-brown glass and steel suggesting a person ought to leave their soul outside on the way in. Importantly, he also noticed that he felt a gnawing, aching loneliness in the centre of his chest every day as he turned the corner back into his street and to his own empty home.

Why had he never noticed these things before? How had he closed down his senses, his perceptions, and his aesthetic responses so much that he could no longer remember what he felt or cared about?

Very few of us in modern life can get through a day with our senses fully awake and responsive. We anaesthetise ourselves with screens and earbuds and medication and constant stimulation and numbing with everything from sugar and caffeine to newsfeeds and Netflix. We are overloaded with junk input and it crowds out so much of our "intelligence" about what we feel, want, need, and see.

Before my camera client burnt out, he had regularly become irrepressibly angry and verbally aggressive with people at work. He described himself as having heightened irritability about the smallest of things – a meeting running five minutes late could lead him to feeling something like righteous fury. He had recently divorced and, in his words at the time, "it cost him half of his life's work" financially. He doubled down on "performance" and expected everyone else to do so as well. He felt utterly bitter. "What a waste," he said.

He thought that the issue was that he was pissed off. It wasn't until he started walking and noticing the outer world again through his camera that he could register the sadness he carried, his loneliness, and, most importantly, his *disconnection from all else*. He was severed from all the non-performance, non-gain-centred ways of feeling alive that he had felt as a younger man, all his other appetites and loves and interests, and something about the small, unimportant, and temporary task of walking and photographing had allowed him to reconnect not just with himself, but with the world he was part of, the world that he was alive in. He recognised that he was silencing the part of himself that was screaming for connection to the world. He had to let the silencer go.

You can do the same.

Open Your Heart

Can you imagine building the habit of checking in with yourself, as you are today? Can you imagine learning to feel into your state and asking your heart what the state of play is? Perhaps you are used to looking outside for answers. Indeed, you, like many people, might outsource the whole thing to other experts and data and never turn your attention inwards for guidance. You are always in process, always flowing and "aliving", and connecting with your state in the moment allows you to ask, "What do I feel inside?", "What is calling me that I am silencing?", "What does this heaviness/fluttering/restlessness I feel want me to know?"

Maybe you are still holding anxiety from your day and you want to move it. What do you feel (not just think) you might respond to? Could something somatic like stretching or swaying, with your eyes closed, work for you? Can you express what is there with a movement if a word doesn't form easily for you? Perhaps you have some sadness in your chest and you want to soothe it; could something warm like a hot drink sipped slowly enough to fully taste it and feel it moving through your throat help to soothe? Or, for you, it might be listening to a mellow piece of music, to every spiral of rhythm and sound that might move you in the right direction.

Your answers will come from your intuition, your nervous system, and especially your heart, and it may take you a while to get used to listening to this intelligence because we have largely closed it down in modern life. When you do tune in, tread quietly, move slowly. Don't allow the loud critics of shame or embarrassment to strip you of your connection to your own needs if swaying sounds too weird or expressing through movement too foreign. No one is watching. Self-permission is so key in this journey. And permission to not always stick to "the rules" is utterly different to not giving a shit about anything. It is far from passive – in fact, it is active and brave, and it really does take discipline. This kind of self-permission is the permission to be whole and responsive, rather than compartmentalised and obedient to embarrassment.

For example, maybe it's a full moon on a night when sleep evades you and you feel disrupted and unsettled by the shifted magnetic pull on the earth and its effect on your circadian rhythms and melatonin production, even though you can't explain why and nothing is *proven* scientifically. There it is again … you feel *silly*. Irrational.

Put one hand on your belly and one hand on your heart and *feel what's there for you*. Explore, without the requirement for validation from external experts. No judgement. Take a few slow moments to notice yourself. What word would you put to that feeling that is keeping you from sleep? What kind of energy is there? Is your nervous system activated or flat? What would you like to do to put the day to bed before you put yourself to bed and let go a little? If you acted honestly in favour of yourself, without fear, and if you trusted your own gut, how would you respond?

Your thinking mind might have all manner of protests to make about this kind of non-rational reflection. Embrace the non-rational for a minute – rewild your psychology. If it calls you, go outside and look at that moon, stand outside in your inside slippers and bathe in it, breathe, be there with it openly, willingly, even if you feel like an idiot. Give yourself the permission to respond to your own intuition and feeling and not be caged by conformity to someone else's idea of what's OK or "normal". Say out loud what you feel (not think) in your body and what sensations you have on your skin and in your gut. Notice who else is there with you in the moonlight. Are there birds or bats or insects or traffic? What scents are wafting up from the ground and what noises thrum in your ears?

Then, you might speak what thoughts are arriving and let them go (especially the ones that say people are probably looking and thinking you are unhinged). You are the only person responsible for your integrity, and you can trust yourself more than you can trust anyone else on this blue planet, there in the moonlight. There is just more of you to explore. Allow a tiny moment of freedom for yourself, and see how it feels.

This little, oft-repeated process of recognising yourself and rewilding your psychology is vitally powerful. Remember: get back to basics; actively let go of doubt and judgement by quietening the mind; slow down for a moment, pause the busyness and let things settle in your mind; reconnect to self through body and senses by listening to what is here; and reconnect to the world that holds you by opening the heart.

You need to be able to experience the sense of curiosity, wonder, and hope that lives within you, and between you and the world, but you have to give up a lot of thoughts and ideas that you've burdened yourself with, crowded your mind with, about what makes you successful, acceptable, or good. This cannot be done with the thinking mind alone and, in fact, mastery of the mind is impossible without a radical reconnection – a homecoming – to ourselves and to each other. We can't know ourselves or our lives only through the masterful mind.

What does it feel like to you when you feel relaxed in a home, welcomed and familiar? What does it feel like in your body? What kind of energy – mental and physical – do you have when you feel at home? What words might describe the sensation? The same feelings, energies, and sensations can be available to you when you locate and strengthen your sense of home within – your sense of internal sanctuary, shelter, familiarity.

It's a surprisingly big shift to make for most overperformers. But once you start to remember yourself again and literally come to your senses, it's time to get as honest as you possibly can with yourself – and then with others.

7.

GETTING HONEST

Coming undone from overperformance, without falling apart for any longer than necessary, means that alongside reconnecting with the sense of home within yourself and the world around you, it is important to get to the nub of what is causing you to feel restless, uneasy, inexplicably lonely, depleted, or unhappy. It's not enough to crash and try to recover the status quo, because the status quo that takes any of us to burnout, staleness, or stuckness isn't really working. This is about trying not to get there again in another two years by getting more radical (down to the root) now.

As we talked about in Part 1, this is not just personal, it's cultural. This dis-ease and cycle of behaviour that leads to burnout is firmly connected to what we believe is right, good, and normal in mainstream Western society and whether or not we feel we fit snuggly with that – or whether we have to mask, hide, or pretend our way into seeming to be good and normal by overperforming. As you have established, it is that abandonment of the authentic self in order to *seem right* and *seem good enough* that drives us to overperform, over-reach, and over-burden ourselves.

This is truly not your only option.

To step in a different direction that might be truer and more vital for you, you have to be able to see things differently, which opens the door to behaving differently. It is this that helps you get unstuck. It started with looking at the outer and inner cultures we live with, and next is looking at yourself, really looking, and then, critically, feeling without blocking or numbing or avoiding. Once you do witness yourself this way, you can gently, kindly start to speak out loud what you see. As theorist and revolutionary Rosa Luxemburg said, "The most revolutionary thing one can do is always to proclaim loudly what is happening."[39]

But getting honest is surprisingly complex.

What Is It to Be Honest?

The easy thing to do is to consider honesty in terms of moral character and assume it is all a matter of choice, something that people of good character do and people of bad character don't do, and, as a result, something to judge as right or wrong – a simple calculus. In truth, this is an idealised image that few of us can uphold meticulously; not because we don't care to and we think deceit is actually OK – far from it – but because we are constantly navigating a complex world with complex relationships and trying to work out how to seem to fit in and seem to stand out. We can, however, charge ourselves with trying to fulfil the duty of honesty to ourselves and others, once we see clearly. That is something more like authenticity.

In between, and however much we might not like to see ourselves this way, honesty is a fluctuating act based on how much you can and will reveal in any given circumstance. I believe that from the perspective of moving from overperformance and masking to wholebeing and authenticity, getting honest has three parts: not lying, not hiding, and "unforgetting".

Not lying

Not lying can be described as having the courage to tell the truth as you know it, in this case about yourself and your life.

Sometimes, we do just straight-out lie about some small aspect of who we are and what we want or like. We deceive on purpose because there is something to gain, and that can be as innocuous as pretending to like cricket or violin concertos to fit in, ease the small talk with someone new, to show a supportive attitude among a group of people who love something you don't care much about, to please someone, to gain some small advantage or favour and even just to seem agreeable.

Lying can also be about what we leave out of what we say, choosing not to disrupt or rock the boat with hard conversations, or not wanting to deal with an emotional rebuttal of some kind. People who feel strongly about the moral benefits of not telling lies and will answer truthfully if asked directly, might still choose to avoid sharing honestly if it means they won't be able to avoid conflict, for example.

Whenever we lie or omit, we register a little ripple of inauthenticity in our bodies. Mostly, when it is small stuff, we can ignore it as part of our "private world" and not something especially risky. The ripple runs through us nevertheless.

Other times, that deceit runs a bit deeper and for longer, like presenting a version of yourself to a potential date or an employer that isn't quite real – not just embellished, but dishonest; "Everyone does that. No one's profile/résumé is honest," we say. "Everyone plays the game at work to fit in." This might feel a little riskier, and that ripple through the body is slightly stronger and creates a more noticeable tension.

And then there is online life and social media, where many people have come to feel that getting ahead and being enough means performing versions of ourselves that are "elevated", "amplified", a bit shinier, or a bit more interesting than the version that we think (and we know deep down in our bones) we really are. And it is something we do very often.

But we still dismiss all of this as part of our "private knowing" and not something we're likely to get caught out or called out on. No one else knows we are being performative so it doesn't matter, right? Our status needs, our desire to be liked, cared for, to be seen as willing, as successful or important, as attractive or intelligent and valued can make some of these *white lies* feel worth it.

How often we do this to make life easier in some way in the moment! But white lies have needs behind them. White lies are about gain that we don't trust ourselves to be able to achieve otherwise. White lies are passive acceptance of ourselves as out of synch with our own truths and our own essence. Those little embellishments and small deceits compound, normalise, and become invisible to us until we are woven up in a web of pretences that actually takes us away from ourselves. And our bodies notice, even if our minds lock it down into our private world.

This is a hot-house for developing the habit of overperformance: pretending to be what we are *not quite*.

The Māori people of New Zealand have a term, "Mana", which is about the honesty and essence you can feel in a living being, an object, or a place. Mana is a term that signifies spiritual power, prestige, authority, and influence. It doesn't have to have anything to do with being "boss" or "big" or even a talker; in fact, it is often quiet, and yet vast. Mana can be experienced in a rock face or a human presence. You cannot fake Mana. It is an impersonal force, an energy that permeates and radiates when it is there, and if it is not there, it is not there. According to the Māori tradition, Mana can be inherited, acquired, or taken away according to one's actions, especially honour, respect, and personal presence or charisma. It is something a person has when they are in integrity and open to life, and not something that they can seek, chase, or achieve in a state of scarcity and fear. It is something whole. Mana inhabits a person who is real and whole. To me, Mana is an exceptionally powerful way to understand the feeling of authenticity, not least because in humans it is never set or "signed off" as an immovable fact; it is always in process, always regenerating through relationship and context.

Likewise, Dr Gregory Cajete, a Tewa author and educator on indigenous perspectives in science, education, and well-being from Santa Clara Pueblo, New Mexico, teaches us about the Native American idea of "finding face (identity), finding heart (passion) and finding foundation (vocation)" in his book *Look to the Mountain: An Ecology of Indigenous Education*.[40] The concept of finding face is about forming a true identity based on the merging of your inner and outer worlds: your character and your context; your sense of yourself as kindred with the rest of the living and inanimate world; and the sense of yourself as part of lineage – a long line of ancestors and a long line of descendants. The concept is about becoming whole in multiple directions, backwards to history and forwards to future kin, upwards to spirit and downwards to earth and place, outwards to culture and behaviour and inwards to character and being-ness. Finding face is a process of maturing, surrendering, challenging, and opening.

Casual dishonesty is a force that takes us away from Mana or from finding face. Even well-intentioned white lies prevent us from allowing truth and authenticity to live in us.

When you do see these white lies, it is important to chip away carefully at them, like carving a truthful portrait out of a block of marble. Don't hack it – self-compassion is important here. It certainly takes a lot of courage to say out loud what you realise about your own less-than-fully-honest behaviours and approaches when those behaviours and approaches may be, in part, the cause of some of your struggles. Remember, burnout is caused by consistently giving your energy and time to people, spaces, stories, and tasks that drain you, without standing for yourself. And that can include giving your energy to pretending. You are not alone in this – not alone in your white lies or pretending, and not alone when you do start to reclaim a better, more regenerative way.

Does asking yourself, "What role do I play in the pattern of depletion I experience?" inspire a little spike of discomfort in you? A defensive reaction? It's often noticeable when we hear ourselves talking disparagingly about what "they" do (the bad workplace, the non-communicative partner) and rationalising what "we" do. Are you able to see some places where you yourself don't stand for your wholebeing? Where you might embellish to impress or mask to conform and fit in?

Is it more comfortable to stick with the story that keeps you free of the burden of having to take responsibility for things like self-care choices? ("They just keep me attached to a screen all day.") What about better boundaries? ("He made me into a hyper-vigilant woman.")

And how do you handle those truths that you don't want to share because they might offend someone close or make you seem like a bad person? Do you actually like working 60 hours a week more than you like hanging out at home, because you are truly really into what you do for a living, but what you say is, "I don't have a choice otherwise I would be here with you"? Do you actually want to be away as much as you are with work demands, because you love something about the solitude or the collegial relationships, for example, but you don't want to admit that to your partner? These are tough truths to face. This kind of honesty well and truly takes you into vulnerable spaces, because, well … who wants someone to think *less* of them?

What I want to say here is that getting honest will need you to compost that thought about being any kind of *less*. It is just too binary, too rigid to be useful. And it immediately leads to shame or fixing.

This is about exploring, excavating, and learning – and self-criticism is the weakest tool you can use to forge a more honest path. Courage, compassion, and vulnerability are the strongest tools for this job. And it is with those tools that you will have to uproot the familiar, less-than-honest stuff to make space for planting the more-honest stuff. We are psychologically composting, not judging. And the reason for it, is to become more like you. The natural you.

An exercise that might help you start cracking the false mirrors is to actually look at your own face in the mirror. This is harder than it seems for a lot of people. Stand upright and properly look into your own eyes until it's slightly … weird. Look into your eyes, not at them – get beyond noticing the colour or the creases and connect with the person *who sees*. This might take you a moment. Recognise yourself here and ask, "Where in my life do I lie most often about who I really am and what I really want?' (For example, "I lie in my work life/my family/my relationship/my online presence the most.")

Take a moment to see what comes up. No need for analysis or critique. The objective is just to speak what you know out loud at this point.

Then you might ask: "What white lie do I want to catch next time, in order to better stand for myself?"

Again, no need to judge your answer, just see what honesty is there for you today.

Not hiding

The second part of getting honest is not about what you embellish, but about what you keep hidden. This is about allowing yourself to stop masking, withholding, denying, and hiding parts of yourself that you like less or that you feel will be less loveable to others. Ironically, the more outwardly successful and popular a person is, the more amplified the feeling of needing to cover up and hide their "real self" can be. The mask sometimes gets harder to remove for people who are admired in their outer world.

In order to keep hiding, we find ourselves numbing or, again, "faking" – specifically *holding back* parts of ourselves. Fake is a strong and shaming term that no one wants to own, but faking isn't just the domain of imitation, trickery, manipulation, or being counterfeit for self-gain. Faking can also be a veil for pain. The way faking might show up for you might be in denying parts of who you are and what you value in order to seem to fit in. This happens in the social phenomena of "code switching", in which a person switches their social style or negotiates with their identity – in some cases, to avoid discrimination. It is tied to the impression management we looked at in Chapter 2, except in this context of honesty it is specifically about hiding. If some aspect of your identity leaves you in the minority, like being the only woman in the room, you might "put on" a style of interaction that you think will make other people more accepting of you as the odd one out. Or if you are the only person with a child or other carer responsibilities in the room at work, faking might look like withholding that information so that you don't risk seeming less committed.

I think of faking as a fear-based distortion of what is true or real for you. The distortion might help you to be seen a certain way, to not be seen a certain way, to feign enjoyment, satisfaction, dislike, superiority, or indifference, but faking is especially utilised in order to stay safe and self-protect. We use faking as a way to protect our real identities when it doesn't feel OK to share them.

How exhausting that is.

Hiding and repressing parts of ourselves necessarily involves becoming numb to our feelings and numb to our real desires. In his book *On Connection*, Kae Tempest reminds us that numbing is a sane act in a world we no longer know how to navigate and survive (an overperformance world).[41] It's necessary. We do it all day – on the commute, in the shopping mall, in social settings, with oppressive work schedules and massive amounts of stimulation. The numbness allows us to get things done in a state of generalised oblivion. It allows us to stay connected to the false sense of performance and success that money and spending offers. But it doesn't stay in compartments. Then we also do this when kissing our partner and thinking of something entirely different. Numb sex. Numb eating. Numb productivity. Numb purchasing. Getting further and further away from ourselves and each other.

On top of faking and numbing, we often hide our passions, let them wither on the vine because we are obedient to maps and models for successful performance that repress our wholebeing. Sometimes, saying what you really want feels like failing in a world that demands urgent, never-ending linear progress and monetary or status success. Maybe for you it no longer makes sense to keep believing that getting a university degree will lead to a successful life. In fact, maybe you don't really want a job in the traditional sense at all, but it doesn't feel like a valid idea, or a realistic way to find success and make a living, and so you don't speak it. Maybe you don't want to push so hard and feel stretched out so thin across so many areas, missing your kids or watching your parents get older and frailer and not knowing how to be there with them more and balance everything else. Maybe you don't want to be anywhere near your parents or your kids! Whether your passion is for a slow, deep life or a big, fast life, a life in the woods in solitude and peace or a life commuting to the heart of commerce on the Shanghai Maglev doesn't matter. It matters that it feels true for you because a life built on lies, faking, or hiding leads to anxiety.

While on the surface it sounds simple to be in tune with our true desires and needs, the reality is that we are messy and complex and wonderful all at the same time, and we don't always know what we want or who we really are, or what gets stamped out in us as we assimilate into the mainstream. This is where living according to values can be so beneficial. As you cross the threshold from overperformance into regenerative performance and wholebeing, the values you live by are something that might need a shake-up in order to make sense for you now.

Values are cornerstones of the way we conduct ourselves in the world. Most people can reel off what are described as "universal values" (things that are considered to have the same value or worth to all people, and that the majority of people, across demographics, hold in common): things like non-violence, honesty, justice, respect for humanity, or freedom.

Then there are personal or core values that an individual aspires to, which might include things like self-development, loyalty, fairness, determination, gratitude, adventure, friendship, harmony, security, service, excellence – the choice is abundant, and social and familial culture very much drive what we lean towards.

In addition, we are influenced by corporate or institutional values like professionalism, teamwork, leadership, commitment, innovation, trust, and transparency. These are the stated, aspirational ones and, of course, there are other values that are shown in action, but not stated – like profit, power, dominance, self-interest, and glory.

Reflecting on your own values and how they support you, I invite you to get curious;

- How might your values shift if you looked at the best way to live your life without hiding or masking your truth?
- What would you use as your value guides if you wanted to live in a state of wholebeing?
- What values would support you to avoid overperforming and be honest about how you are doing as you perform?
- What values help you feel most "at home", within yourself and within the world?

Here are a few values that you might consider:

Being in integrity

Integrity is a beautiful word for regenerative performance because it means both having the quality of being honest and true, but also the state of being whole and undivided between your inner and outer nature, your inner and outer world. If being in integrity was your value and you lived according to it, you would hold your truth up with both hands and not hide it, even to protect someone else's comfort, even if you were scared of it. You would prioritise your authentic voice because it is from that voice that you speak with the most integrity and in most alignment with your essence – your words and actions could not be divorced from that essence. Being in integrity would mean that you didn't live a life of compartments and careful separation, and that you felt like you in every part of your life; unwilling to sacrifice yourself to appear more palatable and, instead, drawing like minds, fulfilling opportunities, and real relationships towards you with the magnetic force of your realness.

To hold the value of being in integrity is like having an internal democracy where all parts of you get a vote on how you live, including the part that wants to rest. Without it, you may have an internal autocracy with the overperformer in you calling all the shots.

Being in vitality

How would you change your behaviour if what you valued was feeling fully alive, fully animated as a human being; having the kind of resilience, energy, openness, and verve that let you flourish? What would you do differently if your objective was to respond to life from the fullness of your intelligence and capability – the wholeness of your body and mind together, the bone-deep knowing and the lightning-quick thinking? To be in vitality means that you could meet with difficulty or joy equally, knowing that both are impermanent and both will move – because everything moves, everything is in process.

I think that the philosophical concept of Yin and Yang from Chinese Taoism offers a brilliant way to consider being in vitality and how it is a necessary value for regenerative performance. You may know the yin-yang symbol; a closed circle with an s-shape line through it, separating the circle into two equal parts. The black-coloured half is Yin, representing darkness, passivity, rest, the moon, cold, and water, and the white half is Yang, representing light, activity, masculine energy, heat, and sun. Both halves interact and connect to form a dynamic, harmonious system – a mutual whole. Even though there are two distinct sides, they are not totally separate. Inside the black swirl is a white dot, and inside the white swirl is a black dot – a seed of the other that shows that they are not in conflict but essential to each other. There is no heat and activity without the cold and passivity. There is no rest without resurgence. No stillness without movement, no attack without defence, no fullness without emptiness. The way to vitality is through flux and diversity. Similarly, regenerative performance does not mean just slowing down or just doing less, it means flexibility, not stuckness and being static. Valuing being in vitality is accepting that you are worthy of a full life of diverse experiences.

Being in relationship

For me, an unequivocal value for a reclaimed life full of regenerative performance is that life has to be done together. The richness of life is in its sharing – in its familiar encounters and repeated intimacies with those we hold close, but, deeper than that, in the knowing that we are a collective, a humanity that is capable of extraordinary compassion, kindness, and generosity, but also great violence, apathy, and destruction towards ourselves and others.

When we choose to act in a way that prioritises relating, we might see ourselves in another person regardless of superficial differences. We might recognise ourselves and our actions as part of the whole, not separate to it, not observing it from afar.

Being in relationship is what is going to make it possible for you to not just see but also care when you yourself or those around you slip into overperformance, and especially when there is a burnout tipping point heading your way. It is so easy and common to habituate and hide patterns that are damaging and lonely-making for you in the name of getting ahead. Being in relationship makes it likelier that we might say to each other, "Hey, how are you doing, really?" or "What is stopping you from resting, really?"

If we are truly living in relationship, it is in relationship to ourselves, to each other, and to humanity.

Being in flow with life

If you valued being in flow with life, you would notice when it changes. You would notice when the things you used to believe in and understand started to shift, and your value would mean that you prioritised shifting with it. That might be as simple as changing your schedule when the clocks go back or go forward and your daylight hours adjust, but it may also be as complex as changing your consumption habits in the face of a changing climate and resource depletion. Can you see places where you stick to the way you used to do and see things, rather than flowing and changing as life flows and changes?

A value of being in flow with life may also show up when you consider your reasons for performing when you were 20 or 25 and your reasons now. Perhaps they've changed? Do you realise something different about yourself, the world, or what matters most to you? Perhaps you've changed too: physically, psychologically, spiritually. If so, it's time to value being in flow – going with it, rather than trying to hold back the river and stay put, gritting it out. Life moves, you move with it.

Reviewing and renewing your values can give you confidence in your direction and an anchor to hold you steady when you feel like hiding or masking. They act as a spiritual and psychological compass, especially now as you transition away from overperformance and towards regenerative performance.

We do benefit from both anchor and compass when it comes to showing up authentically, not least because we are so complex. None of us, ever, sees and knows themselves or another person fully and factually. We are strangers unto ourselves in so many ways: our deep biases and preferences that we don't recognise but which help us feel like we belong "in the tribe" and others don't; our ego and safety needs that keep us projecting images of ourselves out into the world so regularly that we actually think that those images are really us; our lack of scientific or psychological understanding of how our unconscious and subconscious minds really work – the stuff under the surface in imaginations and dreams and drives that we don't know what to make of, if we even notice them; and, not least, how much we are influenced by our "shadows" – those parts of ourselves (often undesirable or "ugly" parts) that don't fit with that self-image that we have, and so we hide or repress them; we don't want to own them. So don't beat yourself up if you recognise where you white lie or fake or hide. Instead, reclaim and use some more of your innate wisdom to step forward.

If you do decide that you want to try more honesty, you might first feel your not-fully-honest moments in your body – a shift, a cringe, a rush to avoid or close something down, a pull towards, a compulsion, a flash of desire, a spark. Witness it. Cherish it when you notice it. It is such good guidance. What did it whisper to you?

Over time, as you practise more honesty and less hiding, you may also learn to speak on behalf of your whole self a little more often. You will find your throat centre (your willpower), as we say in yoga, and communicate more of your cares, standards, and desires. You might ask, "What more am I prepared to show of myself?" And, "Who can I show more of myself to?" It is in these small shifts that you learn to trust your own voice, bit by bit. And, as we will talk about in Chapter 9, as you find more people with whom you can show up naturally, the more familiar it will become.

Unforgetting

The least obvious, but, for me, the most important part of getting honest is "unforgetting". This is about reconnecting with and reclaiming our own core, or essence.

Our essence is both individual and collective. It is about the things that make us unique and also the things that unify us as human beings, and living beings. Essence is that unbuilt, un-curated part of us that remains at the centre – our home that overperformance takes us far from.

It may be quiet, but it is far from underdeveloped; it is original knowing. It is what you know in your bones rather than in your mind. It is grace. It is what you see in the eyes of an animal who docs not feel the need to perform for you and, when you see it, you know it's energy. Essence is your starting point and your end point.

Essence is not something that we need to learn how to create, it is something that gets revealed to us when we stop performing and pretending, and we sit in honesty. Despite the vast diversity of our personalities, at our essence we share play and curiosity, and also the incessant desire to explore and succeed. To grow. We were never naturally passive in the sense of giving up or giving in, unless, of course, trauma has put us there, frozen in time. But sometimes I think that the day-to-day antidote that some people come up with for our toxic overperforming ways is just to stop and stay stopped. That solution is partial, temporary, and not fully human.

Our species has always taken on challenge and strived to be better where we have the option, but better doesn't have to mean more, superior, exceptional, or separate from – those cultural narratives we explored in Chapter 1. Better is something *essential*, not something material. Something that is as deep as it is high, and certainly something whole. If we are really connected to essence, we can't be overperforming. It is not that we don't want to strive or work or push or sweat or find a way. It's not that we want to turn away from challenge. It's that we have forgotten what kind of striving is meaningful for us. And we have forgotten how *not* to strive sometimes too. So, rather than a big epiphany or moment of personal enlightenment, unforgetting is about becoming familiar and friendly once again with our own traits, quirks, and force of character, and with what is common in our shared humanity. Over-performing is a habituated, compounded forgetting of ourselves. It's time to unforget.

The Akan people of Ghana and Côte d'Ivoire have a concept called Sankofa, which means "going back to retrieve what has been forgotten". Sankofa requires deep introspection and revisiting the past to better understand one's truth and move forward with authenticity. But Sankofa is more than a recall and analysis exercise; it is something that has to be felt through the heart as much as the thinking mind.

A person comes to know their essence through their heart, and the talkative mind is not the best guide to the heart. Unforgetting is making way for your heart to communicate what is true for you; your heart already knows.

Your nervous system is another brilliant guide to environment shifts or shifts in other people. You will have experienced your nervous system and your gut responding to something not quite right or shifted in your environment: when your prey or predator instincts kick in and you feel notably vulnerable or aggressive all of a sudden; when the mood changes in a crowd and you know you need to make a move before trouble starts; when you feel the frequency of the moment shift and the tone change without any words exchanged between two people talking close by you; or when a little red flag goes up to let you know that someone else isn't being fully honest. You can tune in to when you are out of key yourself too: "Oh, I just pretended/performed/embellished … what feeling is here with that action?", "What was I avoiding/resisting/needing?" This is unforgetting; the merging of inside and outside worlds.

When you unforget that your heart, your gut, and your nervous system are also vibrant sources of intelligence about your world, you, within it, have the opportunity to harmonise again. Again, as brilliant and mysterious as the human mind is, it has us mostly inhabiting the future or the past; these other intelligences are vital to incorporate when reclaiming your wholebeing.

The essence that you are looking for is the you before all your labels and categories, before judgements about what you did right and wrong. It's your pilot light; the undying blue flame that was there way back, and is there still when you are ready to return.

Honesty as a Kind of Honouring

I love the idea that getting more honest is a kind of honouring of yourself and of each other, rather than a flaw to correct. In this way, becoming more authentic is a deepening and unifying process, rather than something else to achieve or, worse, just another personal improvement process to get through.

Alongside honouring your own wholebeing, honesty also shows a deep respect to and recognising of your fellow human beings. When we dare to be honest, we are saying, "I too am messy and complex and brilliant all at once" and "I too am learning to let go to truth", and, in doing so, you give permission for others to be more like themselves too.

For many people, it feels high-risk to even talk about themselves and their real needs, beliefs, or desires openly at this socio-political moment, for risk of exclusion and "wokeness ridicule" – in a culture that ever more swiftly divides and dismisses "the other". Getting honest then has a tone of rebellion. Merging your inner and outer worlds is an act of resistance. This is a kind of honouring of the psychological activist in you, the change-bringer that is no longer willing to not be wholly you.

Honouring another person who is opening to more honesty is also a radical act, and one that all of us can support when we see it. In Senegal, where I have family, there is a term *"gungue"* (also spelt *gëngë* or *gëngëlu*) in Wolof, the local dialect. It refers to the act of accompanying or escorting someone, especially in a respectful and protective sense. It can carry connotations of showing someone the way, guiding or helping someone get home. It is a way of showing honour and care, and often you will see people of all ages engaged in *gungue*, from school kids walking their friend halfway   back home as an act of friendship, to elders being escorted slowly and respectfully across streets with serious traffic at rush hour.

My hope is that we can help each other walk home towards authenticity.

Some reflection questions that can help you honour your own honesty can include:

- Where did I say what I really meant this week?
- Where did I feel the tug to avoid honesty this week?
- Where did my nervous system feel calm and harmonised, and where did it feel out of synch this week?
- Who did I feel most real with this week?
- Where did I over-reach/overstretch myself this week?
- Where did I say yes when I felt no this week?
- Where did I silence my heart this week?
- Which emotions did I not find acceptable to share in front of others this week?
- How much "psychological space" do I feel like I've got to be a bit more vulnerable today?

Getting honest is getting vulnerable, and it is a true, brave performance to do it.

But you don't have to unleash all your vulnerability at once. It's best to microdose on vulnerability, especially if you are just coming through burnout. If you managed to say, "You know what, I don't really want to go tonight" or "Hey, I know there is a lot riding on this for you, but I am out of steam right at the moment" or perhaps "I guess I'm not really into cricket and violin concertos after all" – well done. Honour where you are at and what capacity you have right now to shed a little more light, to get a little closer.

Crossing these thresholds is partly about necessary recovery and healing from overperformance and possibly burnout. It also puts you in a place to become a regenerative performer in the future, because living from wholebeing allows you to come full circle in your ambitions and hopes and visions for a full and richly rewarding life.

It doesn't stop at not overperforming; in fact, you may be just coming alive and stepping into those ambitions. The "how" is what will look pretty different, as we look at next.

PART 4.

REGENERATIVE PERFORMANCE

The final part of this book is about how to make the change from overperformance and strain to performing in a way that is not just sustainable, it is regenerative. To regenerate means "to create again". Nothing about this journey says that you will never slip back into overperformance, but, if and when you do, you are more likely to recognise what is happening and you will know what to do differently to avoid staying with the pattern of ignoring yourself and feeling lost in order to push on.

Regeneration is a natural ability in living systems. This is true whether that living system is a human body or a rainforest. When regeneration does not happen, it is because something is blocking it.

We have been thinking about some of the culturally and personally habituated blocks that cause overperformance throughout this book and how to start removing them. Now it is time to turn attention to what you might do instead to generate and regenerate your energy and resilience for the most satisfying performances of your life; performances from your wholebeing.

8.

BETTER REASONS TO PERFORM

We both know that we have to perform in life and, most of the time, I believe we actually want to. And we also know that the words and ideas in these pages about the suffering that comes with overperformance have some clenching truths in them. It's reason enough to make some changes, and a springboard to help with that is to find better reasons to perform.

Sometimes, we get so engrossed in what we are doing that we forget to step back and ask, "Why am I doing this again? Why am I on this track and is it taking me to a place I want to go, in a way that I am happy to travel?" The less we ask, the more normalised – and extreme – our overperformance behaviours become, until the question of why we are doing it seems too obscure to ask. The story of more and the story of being ever-better become untouchable, unquestionable. "Is anyone else feeling a bit lost?" you might quietly ask yourself.

Alongside this, the thronging in our ears and the trembling in our hearts as we watch, hear, and feel the seemingly endless violence, destruction, hatred, and division is sometimes too much to bear, if you are looking. It's no wonder to me that the need to stay anaesthetised can override everything. People find themselves stressed into scarcity, silence, and conformity ("Don't kneel against racism in sport, do what you're paid for and play the game"; "Don't protest against the starvation of people in Gaza, sort your own messed-up life out"). When we are in scarcity, we perform out of lack and fear and pain and the instinctive need to push forward, head down, minding our own business. It is a survival mechanism. "Is anyone else feeling a bit overwhelmed?" you might also ask.

Has it ever crossed your mind that you have more choice in how you spend your life? That you can actually design and decide – if you are prepared to let go of some old ideas about what is necessary and embrace some change. What if you wanted a better reason to perform than "just surviving"? What if you flipped the script and recognised that there is a deeper, more compelling reason for you to get up and invest in performing every day, and that reason is love – the most regenerative force of all.

Love and Kinship

Love is not just an emotion, it is a natural state; a biopsychosocial hardwired drive. It's our reason for being, obscured by all the other reasons we have overlaid and overplayed, reasons that, in the end, all point to the desire for and expression of love, acceptance, and belonging. It might be slightly squashed under a big pile of other more negative and more urgent-seeming stuff and a lot of noise, but it's there, waiting for you to recentre it.

We are wired to belong, to connect, to seek each other out and share life. Belonging doesn't have to just be the tribal and exclusive in-group kind that we find within families, teams, friendship groups, and nations, for example, as good as that can be. With an ecological identity, belonging also means, "I, like you, am part of the whole. I am in kinship with everyone and everything else. I am alongside the rest of humanity and the rest of the living world." This kind of love and belonging is about us, not just you and yours, me and mine. This kind is big, wide love and belonging, not small, narrow love and belonging. Both are rewarding, but you can never get kicked out of/divorced from/dropped from "whole" belonging. You can also never turn your head and pretend things are not your problem.

Kinship love is *all of us* love. This kind of love and belonging recentres what is common among us and possible between us, what is precious to us collectively, what matters collectively. And it is my view that when we connect to that kind of kinship love and belonging, our reasons for performing and succeeding in life become so much richer. What you truly want to give your love to, gets wider. "What does my home among my human kin and my home on the planet need me to perform well at?" you might quietly ask.

Every cell in our body responds to love and the adjacent feeling of psychological safety it can bring. But we are equally wired for fear and self-defence, and which of these two templates gets expressed is largely an outcome of the rules of the game we are in. The reason this is so critical to take a look at is that "the game" is actually something that you have more freedom within than you might think. You can participate in your own evolution, our collective evolution, more than you might think, by recentring the regenerative forces of love and kinship. "What in life most needs performance that is fuelled by love right now?" you might wonder.

My proposition to you is that many overperformers are not fuelled mostly by love and kinship. It might look like love on the surface, but the clue is in whether it feels open and self-renewing, about sharing the struggles and the upsides, or whether it feels rigid and a little forced, about protecting what you've got. Someone once asked me, "If you are fortunate, will you build a bigger table or a higher fence?" It is a powerful question, and I know for me which of those would give me the stronger sense of kinship, belonging, and love, and the better fuel for performance. Love is not always the reason we take the risks, push the boundaries, untangle the problems, or make the effort. But I think it should be.

And so I find myself asking some important inflection-point questions to work out just what it is that might re-enchant you to perform *at life, for life, with life*, in the name of love, not fear. As you reflect on the questions that follow, ask your heart and your gut to respond, as well as your mind. My invitation to you is to ask yourself a couple of these questions every morning for a week initially. Write down or record your answers so that you might go back and witness them, noticing what changes as you delve a little deeper each day or one particular question calls for your attention in the moment.

- What is it that you love most?
- Where do you feel most loved?
- What are you ambitious for at this point, and how has this changed over time?
- How does that ambition serve your relationships of care with other people?
- How does that ambition serve your sense of belonging and connection to the world and the web of life?
- What do you put the most performance energy into in your life?
- What do you think is worth giving your priority, time, and energy to, and are those things the same as where you put your performance energy today?
- If you're fighting, what is it that you love that you fight for?
- If you're striving, what is it that you love that you strive for?
- Who do you perform for?
- Who do you most want to notice your performances?
- Who do you most want to perform alongside?
- What does it feel like for you when your performances have got love in them versus when they are fear-filled and come from a place of scarcity?

Rumi said, "When you do things from your soul, you feel a river moving in you, a joy."[42] It is the same with performances; when they are close to your intention, your values, and what it is that you want to give your love to, they flow and feel strong and enduring, whether you are packing your kid's lunch or running a company. It has nothing to do with how hard it is, how much challenge and struggle it requires from you, how much success or failure you have faced, or even whether you think you can really pull it off. You are way more capable than you even think. The question is, what makes you feel aligned and alive?

When we are performative though, which is where we perform so that others see us in a particular way, and especially when we perform parts of our identity that don't feel quite true for us (but we think are expected), the opposite happens. The vitality fades, we drift from our values, our real self stays hidden, and we risk becoming exhausted.

Do you need to be so rough on yourself? Perhaps now is a time for the humility, vulnerability, and courage it takes to sit with these questions and be OK for a minute to not know all the answers, while you learn about yourself anew. This is a time for acting from the heart, perhaps with some refreshed ideas, perhaps with a new view, and definitely with some behaviours that counter the culture that you have absorbed as necessary for success.

Finding better reasons to perform than how you are seen, what you might miss, whether you are running quick enough to avoid failing and falling behind is a sane act in a world obsessed with more. But let's take a look at how it feels – refreshing or depleting – if you think about performances that amplify love; performances that deepen your reciprocity with others and sharpen your presence in today. Let's see how it feels if the map of your future gets drawn up by these coordinates, and not by the tired and tatty cartographers of your go-faster and do-more overperforming past.

Countercultural Acts:
Doing It for Each Other

I don't think there has ever been a more important time for amazing performance than now, but it's a matter of turning our attention to what really needs our performance. The question of how we want to live on the planet together is, shall we say, the most pressing question we have. The psychotherapist, coach, and author Prentis Hemphill asks us to make decisions that do not increase suffering.[43] What a brilliant anchor that is for choosing what we want to perform at.

Imagine if we could make our shared world the primary focus – the "us" of a shared planet and the "we" of shared humanity. Imagine if we could approach that with the developing maturity of people who are also doing the "inner work" of becoming increasingly willing to allow themselves to be whole and fully human instead of machine-like cogs in "bigness and greatness" systems that never stop. However small you feel your role is, it matters how you play it, and what your reason is for doing it well.

Imagine if we could recentre and reharmonise our professional performances so that we are caring for the world in which we live and are part of (ecology) *and* caring for the quality of our way of life (economy). The words ecology and economy both have their etymological roots in the old Greek *"oikos"*, which means "house". Ecology focuses on earth as our home and how we find an appropriate way to dwell on it, and economy focuses on the way we get along in this world-home and with the family of society.

Our interactions with the house that is the planet and the house that is work can be a source of deep fulfilment or an empty transaction. They can never really be separate; our performances in work can never not involve and mirror the world we live in. And so, what needs our attention, our strongest love, in these houses and homes of ours? How will we act for the "us", not just the "me"?

Regathering as an "us", not just a "me"

The seemingly countercultural act of doing things together, doing things for others – especially others we don't know – is a way of honouring life, seeking life, and acting for life outside of our own bubbles. The simple question of whether our performances today act to ease loneliness and deepen connection – for ourselves and others – or perpetuate and recycle the loneliest time we have ever known, can give us guidance. We are part of living webs and living systems, and however far we can get as one person, we don't live (healthily) as one person. Something psychological would always be missing to work only on ourselves. Sure, that's where the work of maturing starts – within you – but if the motivation remains as the betterment of "me", rather than the betterment of "us", we quickly feel untethered and thirsty for something that we can't quite explain … it is love, kinship, and connection.

In part, what I am describing here is community. A kind of regathering of our collective lives. The verb "regather" means to bring together once more or to come together anew; to become whole again. It also means to summon up (something like one's courage) again. Maybe that courage is needed for us to come out of our private and separate mental arenas and *go together*.

Overperformance isn't an organisational problem, a societal problem, or a personal problem – it's a relational problem. To paraphrase author bell hooks, there is a dangerous narcissism that comes from so much attention to individual self-improvement and so little to the practice of love within the context of community.[44]

Our Western narratives and systems do not foster community. They foster independent, individual, or small family units and purposeful teams, perhaps because they are more industrially efficient. Beyond the focus on "me", there is the focus on the bigger circle of "we" – perhaps your family or your team. These can be a powerful container for growth, love, belonging, achievement, and resilience. Families and teams serve a strong purpose in society, and can be a deep and abiding part of our own psychological well-being. But in the absence of community and broader relationships, the family unit or even the team can become burdened with huge amounts of pressure to fulfil too many of the interpersonal needs we each have for intimacy, feedback, support, challenge, and love.

If we are lucky enough, we also have deep personal friendships, and they are the sustaining source for many of us when the going gets tough and, indeed, when everything is great. But most friendships are not intergenerational. They are relationships forged with people of more or less the same age and stage, usually with similar world views and lifestyles, and while we might be eternally grateful for the compassion and humour found in friendships, they, like families, can sometimes be a cultural echo chamber.

Community, however, is more diverse, less controlled, more randomly configured, and, in some ways, more exposing or demanding. Community looks different for everyone and means something different to everyone. It can be a space for sharing, lifting others, supporting, debating, negotiating, protecting, denying, resisting, providing, and reciprocating; a community is alive in relationships and struggles. It is complicated and organic and it is necessarily *made of many*.

Reclaiming community

You may recognise a few types of community, such as communities of place, of purpose, or of passion, as described by author, podcaster, and teacher Manda Scott.[45]

Communities of place are identified largely by physical proximity and shared experiences based on where people live or spend time. In this kind of community, you show up as you are and, while there may be strong characters with strong views, your belonging isn't contingent on anyone else's blessing. A community of place often comprises multiple generations, and sometimes people who have moved from multiple other places. If you are lucky enough to feel the belonging that comes with a community of place, it is a soul-soothe indeed. In 2023, myself and three of my dearest people opened a community gathering space in our local village. We all lived in close proximity in a remote area – off-grid in the middle of a woodland – and so we had become close. Many chats over many dinners fantasising about having great coffee and supper clubs and music and book clubs and conversational exchanges brought us to the decision that we wanted to create a welcoming space for people to be in community and see what would happen, what might emerge. We started, with no idea and a simple intention to welcome and participate. We repurposed an old bank on the main street and made a well-being (wholebeing) studio upstairs with yoga, breathwork, and Pilates, and a cafe downstairs with huge communal tables, and we asked people what else they might like to do in community. People responded. Soon, the upstairs space also became home to singing groups and poetry nights and climate action group gatherings and artist meet-ups (there are some unbelievable artists and craftspeople who have obviously been hiding in sheds across the region for decades), sharing circles and grief groups and junk-samba bands and seed swaps and run clubs and film nights and gut health workshops and kids' yoga. The cafe is full of hikers and families and singles and professionals and dogs, on their laptops, writing or drawing in journals (not the dogs!), knitting, sharing conversation and food with neighbours known and unknown alike. The team that run it are local, many having never worked in hospitality or events before, many having never washed up, served food, or made a coffee, but handling it with budding confidence and care. Some days, we have had an age span of 55 years in the team between the pot-wash and the food truck. We have been asked to hold space for a wedding, a wake, and a christening, and my most recent favourite moment was a local community member who booked a supper club place for herself, drove 40 minutes to get there, and sat among new friends putting the world to rights for her 82nd birthday. There are laughs and tears, there are health crises and celebrations and transitions, and there is real support between people who have come to care for each other. It has undoubtedly been the most rewarding thing I have ever done to discover and belong with these extraordinary people in this community of place. It is not always easy, but the motivation needed is easy to regenerate. None of us had any idea just how rich the community already was. And communities with characteristics like this one exist in many places, with people who genuinely *live* where they happen to reside.

In communities of purpose there is most often a common goal or objective and common values that unite people, like a professional practice network, a group of engaged educators working together to improve educational practice, or a network of volunteers brought together for a specific purpose such as disaster response or aid provision.

In communities of passion, what unites people is a shared interest, shared values or enthusiasm – think religious groups, philosophy-cafe members, Arsenal supporters, or even a committed audience to an idea-led podcast show or Substack channel. Community membership for all can be compelling, entertaining, a place for exchange of ideas, and feeling heard and valued, and can create a reason for people to build relationships, return frequently, and stay for extended periods – all of which can add to the sense of doing life together.

Performing for future and past

Another countercultural act in a time that seems to so deftly inhibit our ability to think beyond ourselves is to question whether we can consider how our performances will affect our descendants in seven generations, and the seven generations of ancestors who put us here today. This concept, rooted in ancient Haudenosaunee (Iroquois) indigenous philosophy, emphasises our community and intergenerational connections and the responsibility we have to each other. Connection is not something that is reserved for immediate family, or even just for the living. Remembering who we are is a practice that reaches back into ancestry, forwards into ambition, up into values and what we hold sacred, down into roots and history, across to each other, and inwards to the heart and mind.

When we feel supported and not alone, with a constructive, all-life-centric, and value-based direction, humans actually do OK. Despite the doom-filled headlines in the news, I feel that there is still a lot to like about human beings – a lot worth fighting for. Working out how to expand and evolve together, in community, is a worthy venture. Reimagining our future performances is surely something that has to be done collectively, and not within the confines of our individualism alone. I, for one, would rather do it with you.

As the late Pope Francis said: "Rivers do not drink their own water; trees do not eat their own fruit; the sun does not shine on itself and flowers do not spread their fragrance for themselves. Living for others is a rule of nature. We are all born to help each other. No matter how difficult it is … life is good when you are happy, but much better when others are happy because of you."[46]

Countercultural Acts: Doing It for Your Own Fulfilment

Somewhere in the cut and thrust of getting through life, it's easy to forget the point of it all. I would like for you to step off that treadmill, which is possibly set a little too fast, and remember what it's like to move freely. Can you notice again that voice in your head that tells you that moving freely is for "after" the performing? That fulfilment is a lucky by-product of an industrially successful life? Or that creativity is a nice-to-have add-on, but competitive dominance is a need-to-have? Your fulfilment is a result of living from wholebeing; a result of expressing your full humanness – that seems to me to be a brilliant reason to perform.

So, what might you focus on if your reasons for performing were about your own fulfilment? A good start would be to reclaim what is natural to you.

Focus on the teachings of competition

The Tarahumara people (also known as Rarámuri) are famous for their incredible endurance as runners. They live in the Sierra Madre Occidental Mountain Range of Mexico, and they have developed a strong tradition of running for various purposes, including hunting, inter-village communication, and ceremonial events, but they also run as competition.

In long-distance races, their physical and mental resilience is extraordinary, sometimes seeing them cover hundreds of miles in a few days wearing their traditional *huaraches* (sandals). What is fascinating about the Tarahumara runners is their motive when they run competitively. These athletes run not so much to win or get a prize for themselves or for personal glory, but to apply all of their strength, will, and spirit to what they see as a "gathering of life"; a collecting up of knowledge and wisdom for their people, so that it might help them understand how to meet the trials and tribulations of living in the times to come. They use challenge as a way of understanding themselves and life, and sharing that with others. It is about fullness, wholeness, and preparedness as a people. It is about expansion to wholeness, rather than reduction to titles, statistics, miles clocked, or individual accolades.

The original Olympic creed could be seen as similarly focused on wholeness and fullness, with the values expressed first as encouraging effort, preserving human dignity, and developing harmony.[47] The challenge of competing itself was the place for development of these values, as it was with the ancient games that valued "noble competition". Of course, this perspective is still visible in much sport and performance today, but there are also many places where we have emaciated the concept of competition right down to a form of dominance and bettering that profits the few.

What will it take to reclaim competition as a place for learning fullness and wholeness versus a place for indoctrination into old ways, elitism, and rigged systems?

If you are not actually scrambling for resources or fighting for your life, human competition, in essence, is about testing our capabilities, your depth and your possibilities, especially your ability to cope; an essential human factor – and when you are really performing at your peak, you have gone beyond coping with competition pressure to having a sense of freedom, whoever you are competing against. Competition is really an inside job. It's an internal phenomenon naturally engineered to make us go further towards the best expression of ourselves.

Yet competition is most often measured by conquest over another. It represents things like defeating, superiority, supremacy, or rivalry, and is focused on the scarcity of resources and territory. In this form, competition represents a high risk of negative outcome, and it has the draining energy of division and superiority. It can be immediately aggressive in this form, and it's easy to see why people might want to turn away from it or feel that it is so limiting. But challenge and competition are completely natural to us. We can meet them with ingenuity, subtleness, smart choices, adaptability, effort, imagination, intelligence, and an open heart.

Competition essentially involves the challenges of winning and losing, both of which are vital states to experience in our psychological growth. It is just about the richest learning ground we can have – if we are genuinely open to learning, that is, and we haven't already decided that conquest and pain are the only curriculum and win or loss is the only result.

Competition doesn't have to be something to endure doggedly with a creed of suffering and sacrifice. When we see competition as a method of maturing and rounding out, each moment of contest gives us the possibility to expand, to understand more, to try something else. Other competitors are simply journeymen and mirror-holders. If we obsess and focus on them, not only do we miss our own growth, we likely do so as a way to channel fear, and then never have quite enough presence left to relish the performances themselves. We have the option to focus on the brilliance, talent, and ability to cope that other competitors show and let ourselves rise alongside it, rise with it – a totally different energy to bring to our performances, even if they are tough days.

I think that competition is not something to be denied but to be completely realigned in its use. It doesn't work to pretend that competition is bad and needs avoiding, that everyone gets a medal for participation and no one mentions the winner. Competition can be fulfilling if we just use it well.

We cannot find all of ourselves if we resist competition – those edges and rough spots and quirks of character, flashes of anger or passion, the cheeky thrill of excelling, or the sharpness of persistence. We are made of this stuff. Even coming back from an overperformance crash will require a kind of competition – the question is, what kind?

I think that we have set the competitive compass the wrong way, a way that only shows one side of competition: a zone of comparison and judgement, a zone for seeking to separate ourselves apart from others, and a zone where avoiding failure and being on top rules the roost.

Alternative expressions of competition are more like a form of discovery of one's own talents or gifts, and the pursuit of depth and mastery of those gifts is part of knowing and sharing who we are as humans. Those performers who manage to compete without a sense of "rightness and superiority" or "wrongness and inferiority" in their outcomes are free to throw all of their fierceness and passion and capability at the contest for the sheer experience of themselves as a human, an uncaged and clever animal that broke out of the zoo of cultural expectations.

Competition is an expression of our real species-ness, our wildness. Like facing and overcoming challenge, competition can teach us how to "do life"; how to design life. It is as important to our fulfilment as any other human factor. Our question, always, is how we use it. Because we are not just competitive by nature, we live in a climate of competition; a scarcity system.

Ask yourself, what would it take for me to see competition as transformational and fulfilling, rather than threatening? How can I shift to see challenge as a necessary good – part of finding fulfilment and truly relishing my performances, rather than a necessary evil to get through?

Focus on your natural creativity

"I'm not a creative person," I heard a young person I care about say as she closed her laptop and put down her phone after finding 20 ways to travel across Europe for minimum cost, including the places she'd swap books, clothes, go solo, link up, adventure, recoup, work, play, swim, meet, host, give, receive. She was designing her life.

"I remember drawing a horse when I was a kid and it was really terrible. My poor mum put it on her wall at work and had to look at it, but my dad told me how crap it was and I realised I just wasn't creative."

I watched this kid perform on stage in front of hundreds of people, sing her heart out to a pin-drop silent crowd and let herself follow the music she was making as it expanded to fill the whole building, despite shaking in her 10-year-old shoes. I watched her balance work and study through Covid, solve problems all day long working in cafes and restaurants and office jobs, shimmer laughter out at her own human flaws, find her feet again after low moments and disappointments, regenerate her own energy after illness, and still keep her lovely green eyes on the possibilities in front of her.

Creativity is not about being able to draw a horse, or any other artistic pursuit. Creativity is a profound way of responding to everyday experiences with diversity, confidence, and self-awareness. It is not just a talent reserved for the artistic or the preserve of professional creatives – even boredom can inspire a creative rumble in us, some necessary movement to avoid the static. It is a fundamental performance practice; an enticing way of doing life for anyone.

I especially love record producer Rick Rubin's take on creativity as the channelling and embracing of our natural inclinations and vulnerabilities.[48] That take relies on us listening to our own intuitions, ideas, and instincts – trusting our guts and our "inner listening" and being willing to follow whatever spirals and diverse plot twists arise without shutting ourselves down before we have explored and expanded. Creativity is movement, fluidity. The schoolishness we spoke about in Chapter 1 encourages us to choose one thing that is correct and stop there, perfecting and defending the performance of *that* thing with no room for any more "ands".

But what feels right and resonant inside will likely resonate best outside too. What is interesting to you will likely result in the best outward performances, because if you can keep yourself inspired (a word that originally came from "breathing in the divine"), there will be a quality of realness in what you do, a quality of authenticity that is way richer than anything you could mimic that someone else does. Trust your own inspiration. You can't "perform yourself" for others and expect to feel fluid and confident.

If you are inspired to build something or make something or tend something, and you feel that it is a kind of distraction from the to-do list, that it's "off-track", think again. That is creativity calling you, inviting you to respond to the spark of connecting pieces or removing what is not needed or changing things to enhance, reveal beauty, embellish, bring joy. The flow of creativity that you find in your "distraction" pulses outwards to your other endeavours and reminds you to move with the energy, not against it. It also pays respect to your intuition and, hey, you might like following that spark.

Liking your own creative practice is a brilliant reason to perform.

Focus on your fulfilment as a necessary practice

Maybe one of the most countercultural acts we can do is to perform for the purpose of fulfilment – a response to the desire in our bellies and dreams in our mind's eye. I believe that is what British climber George Mallory meant when he was asked, "Why do you want to climb Mount Everest?" and he answered, "Because it's there."[49]

Fulfilment is seen as an ultimate reward, a thing we might get later, rather than something that should be on the balance sheet that rules our lives every month. But imagine if, once you have what you need in basic resources, you could focus on the *trying* that might fulfil you. So deep is the narrative that we have not yet reached the mythical finish line and therefore cannot stop, so strong is the illusion that we are about to fall behind and there is so much more to attain, that we can barely stop to notice whether all of our trying is making sense to us.

For Mallory, the trying that fulfilled him was climbing mountains – that was his medicine. That is what he wanted to perform at, for the sake of it. For me, it is growing things. Pulling out a radish this morning literally turned me into a grinning child again, even though most of what I plant gets eaten by some other garden being before I get to it, and planting trees is something closer to sacred for me, something I can't explain but am compelled by. For my business partner, it is growing people, the patient investment in a young person that helps them "become" and trust themselves, even if they never look back as they rise – that's not the purpose, or the fulfilment, for him. For some of the science clients I work with, it is the joy of invention itself, of breathing life into possibility.

Once again, I invite you to get curious:

- What is it that you want to give your trying to?

- What seduces, invokes, and compels you but doesn't make it to your balance sheet that rules your life today?
- What would your medicine be, the kind of performances that might heal and harmonise your soul?

Reframing your reasons for performing is a powerful act of reclaiming your life from the world of overperformance. One of the roots of the word "reclaim" comes from the 14th-century "reclamer", meaning "to call back a hawk to the glove". In such reframes, you call back what is natural to you in motivations too. All that remains is to develop some new personal, practical approaches, and you have stepped into being a regenerative performer in body, mind, and soul. In the last chapter, we take a look at some of these practices.

9.

THE REGENERATIVE PERFORMER

So, what exactly is a regenerative performer? It is someone who understands that performing with an industrial mentality is less effective, less sustainable, and a worse experience than performing with an ecological mindset. Not only do they understand it, they act accordingly – building practices, habits, and methods that help them regenerate energy, stay aligned, and project their authenticity. If you have recognised yourself as an overperformer throughout this book, the practices in this chapter can help you to make the transition.

Regeneration essentially means continuing through renewal – something more like "to bring forth again", re-establish, renew, replace, or restore things back to their whole, full, or natural state. The body can regenerate damaged tissue, for example, and the tissue will indeed be new, but it will perform the same function as it did before it was damaged.

It's the same with our psychology, including our behaviours around overperformance. The idea isn't to stop performing or lower the bar on finding success; it is to reposition our ideas and actions so that we might come back to being whole and in integrity with ourselves when we perform.

It's not a choice between stop or go, yes or no, perform or quit, it's about how to regenerate yourself as a performer. It's about bringing forth what is naturally within us if we allow ourselves to come out from under the heavy cloud of old narratives, expectations, and ideas and do something else, something that really works for us. It's about doing well and staying whole without needing to choose between the two. It allows for logic and sensuality, practicality and imagination, speed and slowness, intensity and light touch, internal focus and external focus, for "me" and for "us". That is the core of regenerative performance.

Noticing

It often astounds me how much my own thinking has been shaped by the cultural narratives I hold and the systems that keep those narratives in place. Even though I have deep conviction that performance has to be something we regenerate in cycles, often I hear my "old voice" telling me that there are a million other things on my to-do list and they are urgent priorities.

My relationship with rest is especially tricky. I am not a lay-around-and-rest person by nature. The couch and I are not particularly close. I'm excitable and overly optimistic about the things I can get through in a day, and that list is always a bit too long, so I can easily drift to the always-generative without the regenerative part.

But I noticed over the last years how much I cringe when people say, "I know you're really busy but…" How much of that busy was rest-less-ness? I noticed I felt uneasy when people said, "Oh, she's a force of nature." What kind of force? Like a hurricane? A volcano? A tsunami? Or like the compelling pull of the seasons that includes surrendering and slowing as well as growing and producing?

And then I noticed after burnout that my body and mind just don't work well at sprint pace anymore and I feel the depletion much more readily if I do overperform. But they do work well when I invest in renewal and rest, so I started to listen to myself more honestly...

And so, I have had to practise rest, and to make rest a practice that is central in my life – not something I do *after* life happens that day. For me, that has not meant more time on the couch in real terms, or not even any more time on my yoga mat. It has meant being willing to travel a little further from my familiar patterns and enter new territory. Like saying "no thanks" more often. Like valuing the sanctuary of home and its embrace of solitude and intimacy more. Like living in accordance with seasons and cycles as they present themselves, and so knowing that my animal body will likely want to move more slowly after harvest and sniff out newness in the spring. Like resting in the acknowledgement that there is no finish line and I'm right where I should be. And like recognising that it is in stillness, especially, that I come to understand my place in the shifting world and the natural order – the things that really matter, which are way beyond this tiny "me". *That* is truly rest.

The Core Four: Regenerative Performance Principles

Noticing yourself is like pressing the pause button to evaluate. After that, we need to know what to do next. I believe that regenerative performance requires you to truly engage with and regularly enact a few performance principles.

The first is that you need to be able to come to presence regularly so that you can continually check-in on yourself.

The second is that you need to be able to diversify your modes and speeds of operation – moving between what researchers

Dr Megan Reitz and John Higgins call "spacious mode" and "doing mode", for example.[50]

The third is that you need to perform according to your own wild clocks and natural rhythms, and not just the mechanical clocks we are so used to.

And the final principle is that you need to get used to integrating and prioritising your body intelligence in all of your performances in life.

These four core principles allow you to build better, more supportive habits and resist some of the methods and overperforming ways that you are outgrowing. My hope is that in addition to the suggestions here, you will continue to build a playbook of your own against these principles – and add some more of your own.

Come to presence

What is presence? Presence is the quality of internal silence that emerges when you stop trying to know, work it out, predict and plan the future, or analyse the past and start paying attention to what is here, within you and around you, now. It begins with proximity to your surroundings – the feeling of being here in this place, in this moment, with these others.

Presence is really the only way to experience life for ourselves. We are so habituated into checking the weather app on our phones rather than looking up, or checking our fitness tracker rather than connecting to our heart rate or feeling into our bodies. Our need for information input and expert opinion can keep us away from *being here in this moment, with these others.*

Presence isn't something you can force or set goals for; its energy is subtle and won't be bullied. It won't come to you through thought – you come back to it through noticing. It is the ability to lift up out of urgency and future-planning and desires and cravings, and find a potency of attention that is so far superior to the clambering mind, it is scary to think that we've been driving the bus without it.

Un-presence is a form of coping with "too much-ness": too much stimulation, too much to do and achieve, too much hate and division and fear, too much risk of failing – a cocoon of overwhelm that doesn't let up. Add to that the fact that we have come to see ourselves as most worthwhile when we are busy, and suddenly psychological retreat and distraction are no-brainers.

The problem is, of course, that life is now, and being un-present brings constant low-level strain and suffering.

Let me offer a tiny example of the difference between getting stuff done and presence. I keep an organic vegetable and herb garden. In classic overperforming Pippa form, it conists of 15 raised beds, as if I were a market gardener. I do get truly satisfied when I harvest something to eat or a flower to share with someone, but it is also a straight-up learning ground for my own resistance of overperformance and practice of regenerative performance.

Creeping buttercups had become my nemesis. They are all over the herb beds and they are very resilient. It feels like 2 million of them grow overnight, and I noticed that every time I went out to the garden, I would feel the "need to weed", and weeding is like outdoor housework. My mind would disappear into the task and slight grumpiness, and now and then a fleeting "Is it all worth it anyway?" would flash across my mind.

I went out several mornings and stood there, the long task list looming while I procrastinated with my hori-hori knife in hand. But something happened. I stood there long enough to notice the whole community of beings that call this herb bed home. I noticed who ate there, faces buried in pollen or crumbles of soil. I noticed what happened after rainfall as the buttercups pulled the cloak of their petals closer and the robins and song thrushes swooped in for a meal – the same robins and song thrushes each day flamboyantly tossing aside debris to claim their worm. I noticed the devastation that strong wind brought and how all the diners found shelter in crevices and corners or went subterranean. On consecutive dry days, the flowers that normally leant towards the sun became withered and softened and were no longer able to lift their cup to the bees. I became fascinated with the goings-on in the herb beds. I felt no need to analyse or label or "work out" what was happening; it was simple presence and recognition of the life around me. In that state of presence, I could listen to the soft sound of percussion as the rain fell on an upturned bucket. I could hear the gossiping squirrels fussing over a nut. I could notice the cluster of aphids clinging to a rose stem and a violet ink beetle scuttering across pebbles. I could smell the scent of warm earth after rain – petrichor. It was enlivening and sensual. It was healing.

But it wasn't just an observation from "in here" about what's going on "out there". I was recognising myself too, my steady heartbeat, the temperature of my skin. I was still but not static, more like still the way long grass is still; alive-still. I had a sense of also being in that neighbourhood. It was some kind of communion, with no explanations required. The slow and local knowledge felt wondrous – a totally different kind of literacy. I still had the weeding to do, but I was present for it, engaged and involved in doing something that played an important part in the cycle of the garden that I love. I was aware of myself as part of it, and the act felt more like tending than ripping out uninvited plants with irritation. My experience was so different, just by surrendering and sinking into the moment.

Clear, calm attention is like a little window into the intricate relationships that sustain all life. Without attention, I would not notice that the buttercup is never separate from community, climate, or the rhythm of the seasons. Likewise, the spider's web on the gatepost, with its gorgeous orbs of shivering dew, is only strong because it is attached to what is around it. But before we can really see connection or relationship and value them fully, we have to be present, *be alongside.*

You don't need to think your way into the world again, you are already part of it. You already belong to it. You just have to come back to presence to feel that. Presence allows you to step outside that endless conversation going on in your head and into the incredible communication going on between cloud and leaf, foot and ground, skin and sun, laughter and care. Presence is a suspension in the now, in the space between the demands you make on yourself.

If you stop to attend, you might notice that inexplicable pull towards the natural world – even if it just tugs at your shirt sleeve and suggests you get out of the office and into the air for 10 minutes. There is something essential in us that makes us want to test the temperature of the ocean, peer over the edge of a cliff, see what's on the other side of a hill, find where the heavenly scent is coming from, stretch upwards towards the sun, and get sand between our toes. These intuitive whisperings and enchantments are soul calling.

We open space in ourselves not by knowing more, but by deepening presence. It is in that space of presence that we can notice whether we are performing regeneratively or heading for overperformance. Coming to presence might literally involve taking a deep breath in at your desk and asking yourself, "Where is my attention?", and gently bringing it back to follow your next breath.

A client of mine goes outside her office once an hour because, for her, that ritual of moving into fresh air whatever the weather, just for a moment, is her cue to come back to herself and to presence in a frenetic day. "How am I doing?" she asks herself. "What am I feeling?" A footballer I worked with used to wear an elastic band around his wrist and ping it as a cue to come back to presence instead of getting caught up in the stress of the past or future mistakes. He pinged that thing a hundred times a day at first. But the more you do it, the more readily available that state of presence is – on demand. Eventually, he just needed to look at the band, and then he didn't need it at all to experience calm presence.

Diversify your modes and speeds

Sometimes, though, it feels truly difficult to step back and pause. Every fibre of an overperformer sees it as lazy or not optimising, and the default setting is "I can squeeze a bit more value out of myself". Being present or deliberately choosing to open up more space and come out of go-fast mode seem like the opposite of performance.

In that respect, presence and spaciousness have a PR problem. They are both essential performance factors in productive time. They are what allow you to maintain quality and clarity, decide well, see different possibilities, see the macro as well as the micro, and focus without losing perspective.

Regenerative performance is about movement. When we are stuck in relentless doing, sure, there is movement, but it's movement with the energy of anxiety, urgency, or sometimes thrill too, and it's one-way movement. It makes me think of the word "haste" and its root origins, which were struggle or conflict, or even violence in the Old English. Even now, haste means excessive speed.

Excessive. Now there is a word that doesn't gel with regenerative performance. It means more than is needed, normal, or desirable. Excessive takes up all the space. Performing from there, coming up for a gulp of air and going back in for another round, can lead to trampling – over others, over the planet, over yourself. Even when you are doing great work, you need to account for how you are doing it, and it is only spaciousness that really allows for that. Even a person who is deeply invested in one thing, mission-led, endlessly curious, and passionate, still needs space and presence enough to be involved in a relationship with life, for life's sake even if not for theirs.

When we kill the space, we avoid the need to look in the mirror and check ourselves. There is no time left. We also speed past the spaces where doubt could arise, where we might have to feel and acknowledge the overwhelm and the lostness. Whenever I see someone who cannot stop running, will not stop running, who needs – not prefers – to go fast, I wonder what needs healing for them.

On the flip side, some people withdraw so far from doing or pushing that they also get stuck in one-way movement. The demand for too much space is as much a form of avoidance and excess as relentless racing. Shutting out, suffocating, denying entry to anything difficult is equally a form of ego-fragility, something that needs loving attention. Closing down all possibility of disruption to your inner peace is temporary at best, and unsustainable beyond that, if you want to be in relationship with life.

Both relentless doing and rigidly resisting have the flavour of addictive behaviours; coping with life rather than performing with it. Both turn away from wholebeing. Life moves, and we can move with it. A regenerative performer is able to consciously diversify both the speed they move at and the type of "doing" they are engaged with. For example, a client who is on the journey to becoming a regenerative performer recently implemented what she called a "mental movement matrix" for herself. She was regularly getting depleted staying in a fast gear and task mode, trying to catch up with high demands in a new role. She was starting to feel like she was failing, because she was expecting to drag more out of herself while she was already tired and feeling anxious and "dull". With an understanding of the importance of mental movement for her energy, she devised a weekly schedule across four axes:

1. Fast and intense
2. Slow and deliberate
3. Ticking off tasks
4. Deep dives

Each Sunday before her week started anew, she looked at her schedule and overlaid the matrix. An even split wasn't practical, but she could deliberately ensure that there were two deep-dive sessions for at least two hours each in the week, and one hour a day of slow and deliberate time – which often looked like conversation with colleagues or writing documents (previously she had been doing the writing at home after dinner). Her matrix meant she had to say "no" more often and navigate the feeling of disappointing people, but the dynamic balance it gave her was a game changer. When she felt overwhelmed, she knew she was going to be able to change her speed up and change her mode soon. Such a simple change gave her the sense of space she was desperate for.

In their groundbreaking research report on spaciousness, Dr Megan Reitz and John Higgins recommend a practice of "and" and "both", with the skill that we would all benefit from deepening being the ability to *move between* "doing" and "spacious" modes, for both organisational and personal well-being.[51] They offer several compelling insights to developing such skill, including recognising that spaciousness is likely non-verbal (music takes up less room than words in the mind), that organisations need to develop a language of spaciousness to counter the language of busyness that pervades work life, and also that it is spacious mode that we are most likely to need to actively give ourselves permission for because the start point is already very unbalanced in favour of doing mode.

I would add that shifting the physical space that you are in can help to create more spaciousness – it's another way to nudge yourself into movement. Perhaps for you that is going to a "third place" – a term used to describe a publicly accessible space where people gather for social interaction, outside of their home and workplace. It is a place where individuals can connect with others, often over shared interests or activities, without necessarily being associated with the usual routines of home or work. Sometimes, it's as simple as a comfortable coffee shop, and the shared interest is just the feeling of being with others, enjoying the ambience, the coffee, and the welcome without feeling rushed, and without feeling the need to engage in anything particular except the communion and sense of place.

It can be helpful to use your voice to create space too, like saying no when you mean no, as my client had to, and saying definitely yes when you want to say yes. Asking for space is important as well –

naming the need for psychological space in your week without feeling that it is somehow overindulgent.

Finally, I would add that being willing to take up space in order to stay whole is vital. If you find yourself compromising your spaciousness in order to keep up with your boss who is always late and needs to leave early, or your partner who plans three more activities than you want to do at the weekend, name it, compassionately, and invite that person into the idea of movement between modes.

It's important to recognise here that expanding the permission you offer yourself (and others around you) to rest, come to presence, and get into spacious mode cannot just be another extraction exercise to squeeze out more performance. These ways of being, these skills, have value for their own sake too. Most "aliving" happens when we can mature into this kind of wholebeing.

In their report, Reitz and Higgins emphasise too that we can't add spaciousness as a side order to the rest of the working week – a minute's pause here or there before the *real mode* of doing gets started. Spaciousness has to be integral to your "way" of working, otherwise its power is never given a chance.

They quote from A. A. Milne: "Here is Edward Bear, coming downstairs now, bump, bump, bump, on the back of his head, behind Christopher Robin. It is, as far as he knows, the only way of coming downstairs, but sometimes he feels that there really is another way, if only he could stop bumping for a moment and think of it."[52]

In my client group, I spend a lot of time emphasising a concept I learned in elite sport and adapted using ecological principles, which is the perform–rest–renew (PRR) triangle. A triangle is not only one of the strongest and most stable shapes, it is naturally occurring in ecological life and often found at the point where straight upward growth no longer offers sufficient strength or stability, like when a tree starts to branch out. The metaphor of the strong triangle serves as a basis for considering what you actually need in order to reclaim your performances and, more importantly, your life:

- Performance is what we do when we take action towards executing a task, a piece of work, a feat of some kind. When it is done well, we see it as effective, efficient, or achieving a result.
- Rest is what we do when we deep sleep, nap, couch-potato, and watch a movie – rest is when we stop.
- Renewal is what we do when we play, rejuvenate, laugh, express, create for creation's sake, move for movement's sake – renewal is when we let go of achieving and revivify.

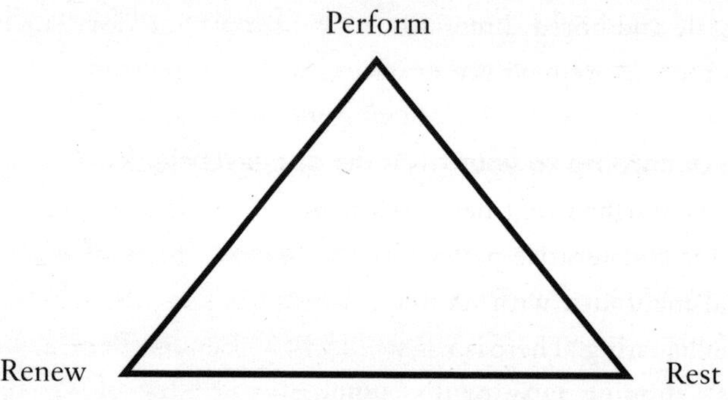

The human body is designed for PRR. As part of its miraculous design, we have something called a parasympathetic nervous system, otherwise known as the "rest and digest" system. It is part of the autonomic nervous system that does its maintenance work without us sending commands like "pick up that spoon" or "open your mouth" or "get ready to respond to danger" that come from the sympathetic nervous system. The parasympathetic nervous system works in the background to calm the body, conserve energy, and perform daily functions like digestion, urination, or salivation when the body is at rest. It slows the heart rate, constricts the pupils, and stimulates gland secretions to restore the body's normal state after stress. It does its best work when we rest and renew: rebuilding, reconnecting, and resetting. If we don't do the resting and renewing well, we don't fully reset, and stress compounds in the body.

The PRR triangle is not about equal time, it's about equal emphasis. It is rarely realistic for us to spend as much time on rest or renewal as we do on productive work in all its forms, but we can shift our mentality to genuinely accept that the time spent on renewal and on rest is time invested in regenerative performance; performance that supports our wholebeing. It is another way to consider how you diversify your speed and your mode to regenerate yourself and your performances without wearing yourself out or getting stale and bored (I remind my clients that boredom is a form of stress too). Movement is everything.

Perform according to your rhythms and wild clocks

We have established that being stuck in one mode, one pace, does nothing for regenerative performance. Likewise, being stuck in the industrial mentality, with its massive emphasis on the scarcity of time, is exhausting. There is rarely a feeling of enough of time – it's flying, it's slipping away, or it's running out. Problems are ticking time bombs or time sucks. Sometimes, time is dragging or we're stuck in it. We use language like "unscheduled time" or "owning your own time" or "racing against the clock"; we commit to "making time" for things and we expect not to have our "time wasted". Time, or rather clock-time, is a container in which we live our whole existence, measuring, organising, and coordinating productivity. We might never really consider that it is a human-made phenomenon designed to help us not choke.

Sometimes, we feel like time is "suspended", and we can step outside of its tight grip and be transported elsewhere, to somewhere or something timeless, somewhere so essential or good that it isn't affected by the tick-tock of productivity. I don't think a sole focus on clock-time is enough to bring us to wholebeing or help us perform regeneratively. Time scarcity is a kind of impoverishment that can affect us on every level of our being, and we need to be able to be here, now, thinking much bigger, without the ticking.

There is also geological time: eras, periods, epochs, and ages. Geo means rock, and geological time is the only way to think about how long it takes for a rock to form or to be turned to sand, how long it takes a pebble to be worn smooth by water, a glacier to melt, a valley to carve out, a landscape to write its own story. Thinking in geological time now and then is an exercise in perspective and how relevant our today-worries are, but I still don't think it's enough to guide us to regenerative performance.

Beyond the mechanism of clocks and eras, though, lies the miraculous fluidity of the present natural world. This is another kind of movement altogether, something that is much more like *rhythms*. The ocean's rhythms are waves and peaks and lulls and ebbs that are part of tidal rhythms; the moon's rhythms involve waxing and waning; and the sun's rhythms involve setting and rising. Each of these rhythms is a cyclical pattern in nature that influences the behaviour and survival of both plants and animals. Nested within the life cycle of a young female tree is an annual cycle of growth and rest that can play out for centuries, favouring long periods of rest, and a faster cycle of collaborating with day and night and season that allows her to respond to the conditions around her in order to flourish. These rhythms are crucial for the health and well-being of the planet's ecosystems and the creatures that inhabit them – including us.

The circadian rhythm is the most fundamental natural rhythm, driven by the earth's rotation that creates night and day. Plants and animals have evolved to synchronise their physiological processes with this rhythm, influencing sleep and wake cycles, feeding patterns, and various other biological functions such as hormone production, body temperature, and more. The circadian rhythm is influenced by things like lights, noise, types and timing of food, and interaction with others – all of which help "reset" the "internal clock". How close to natural circadian rhythms are you, in this modern life of waking, eating, and resting to the clocks of industry, constant pseudo-social interaction, global time-zone blindness, and artificial light from your screen?

For some creatures, a biological rhythm called "infradian rhythm" (a biological cycle that takes longer than 24 hours to complete) also plays a big role in their health and performance, and an example of this is the menstrual cycle, which occurs approximately every 28 days in women and some primates like macaques, every 29–35 days in orangutans, gorillas, and bonobos, every 33 days in bats, every 12 days in an elephant shrew, and for the lucky spiny mouse, every 9 days. For humans, toothed whales like orcas and short-finned pilot whales, belugas and narwhals, and possibly elephants and chimpanzees too, menopause is part of that natural infradian rhythm, an indication of a period of new, differentiated activity and physiological needs – in all but humans who expect business as usual. If you are a woman, have you noticed how different your ability to regenerate your energy is around your menstrual cycle, and how perhaps you expect the same output from yourself as at any other time? How hard it is to honour your body and your energy as it fluctuates in systems that demand constant industry? If you are a woman who has reached perimenopause or menopause, have you found it hard to explain just how different you feel, how much editing of your real needs and feelings you have to do to conform to the norm? Your natural energetic rhythm has changed, but the system you are in isn't usually kind to such changes. How can you honour your energetic needs, for now – for this time?

An example of this could be something like the creation of a "nap room" at work for parents returning from maternal and paternal leave, recognising that sleep is probably in short supply for new parents, and a 30-minute nap could regenerate energy in a way that three more coffees would not. That is smart ecological thinking.

Likewise, seasonal rhythms, driven by the earth's yearly cycle, result in the alternating seasons of spring, summer, autumn, and winter. Different latitudes experience very different seasonal changes, including variations in temperature or day length, for example, and that in turn affects how much growth happens in plants, whether animals migrate to warmer climates or adapt for different conditions by adding weight or shedding winter coats. The adjustment made by living beings to meet their environment and flourish has always been associated with the rhythms of the earth – these are the traits that enable living things to coordinate their way of life with the world around them. Until recently, that is.

In a brilliant essay called "Wild Clocks", environmentalist and writer David Farrier explored how these rhythms of nature are falling out of synch, in part as a response to climate change.[53] Farrier uses the metaphor of wild clocks to describe the biological rhythm of all living organisms, rhythms that drive life forward hour by hour, day by day, season by season.

He talks about how these wild clocks are increasingly misaligned with each other and their environments. Plants are losing touch with their pollinators because flowers bloom too early. Predators and prey are misaligned in timing, creating overpopulation in some species and lack of food for others. Breeding seasons are starting to fail more often in changed conditions. At the very bottom of the oceanic food chain, plankton blooms are becoming shorter due to warming seas. These ancient relationships that weave things together through shared need are out of synch.

Perhaps our own wild clocks are out of synch too.

Time lives in the body not as the mechanical tick of a clock, but as a pulse in the blood, a thought deep in our genetic memory, and a complex melody of tempos and rhythms that lift us into peak performances and rest us back into moments of renewal. It is a stark contrast to the mechanical tick-tock of the clock that we respond to – the bleep of alarms and calendar prompts and deadline reminders that serve our industry and not our ecology. We, too, are nested in cycles and seasons, but ones that we have forgotten.

As a regenerative performer, you will undoubtedly have, and hopefully relish, periods of great momentum and industry, periods where you are willing to take big risks in exchange for big rewards, periods of pulsing with productive energy and vibrancy. Hard periods where resources are not so abundant and you need to be extra attentive, and periods where your performance is fertile and you really want to get out there and among the action. You will also have periods of shedding, letting go of what no longer serves you so that you can move, transition, and adapt. There are also periods of dormancy, what author Katherine May has called "wintering", where we turn our attention inwards to rekindle internal fires.[54]

No summer lasts forever, and forcing the same level of energy and output from yourself is denying life's own rhythms of performance. Those disruptive energies that call you to move and lift or to slow and shed or to turn inwards to depth are the energies that push you closer to wholebeing and regenerative performance.

So much of the mainstream well-being and performance conversation is about balance, and sometimes that idea of balance gets confused with stasis, stillness, and steadiness. Anyone who has ever tried to stand on one leg and lean forward will know that balancing requires dozens of tiny movements and adjustments – wobbles in my case. It is always dynamic and shifting. We don't have to find the middle ground between total stillness or slowness – we need diversity, movement, and regular adjustment.

I was discussing rhythm with a client recently who has been exploring what works for him after initially resisting the idea of more rest or regeneration as "impractical" given his tremendous workload. A thoughtful, intelligent guy, he had been feeling pretty flat about "not keeping up" in his professional world and was seriously thinking about giving up some of the work that was most time-consuming but which he was most passionate about. He was conflicted and fed up, and when I asked him to consider how rhythm worked in his life, he looked dubious. He didn't think about rhythm, just output, he said. But, despite his doubts, he brought forward the image of the grandfather clock that his own grandfather had left to him and to which he was very attached. It was solid, steady, never missing a beat. "The clock keeps rhythm," he told me, "it is always the same, always steady." He knew that the metronome or pendulum inside the clock gave it its constancy. As he paid more attention to the way the grandfather clock held its rhythm, though, he noticed that while the time that it took for one complete pendulum swing from left to right was always the same, the pace of the pendulum varied a lot. At the top of the swing the pace was much slower than when the pendulum swung through the bottom. "It is constant," he said, "but the pace actually changes loads to get that constancy." Exactly!

When you think about your natural rhythms, what do you notice about pauses, ebbs and flows, steady beats and skipping beats across a year? Is your spring energy different to your Christmas energy? Is your 9pm energy different to your 10am energy? How can you honour these natural rhythms and work with them to stay regenerative, rather than extracting more out of yourself because the industrial clock tells you *it's time*?

Integrate your body intelligence in your performances

Your body tells you everything you need to know about regenerative performance. The problem, of course, is that we have almost entirely forgotten how to listen to it. This fourth principle is about embodiment – reclaiming your body as an equal centre of intelligence in your life.

Your body will show you a "live dashboard" reading of whether you are depleting or regenerating your energy at any time. It will offer you a set of indicators and monitors and go signs and stop signs right now, like a sensory guide to help direct you. Is your tongue resting in the mouth or your jaw clenched? How is the level of tension in your neck? Do you feel like your lungs are full of oxygen, or is the CO2 a little high in this closed room with seven other people after an hour? Is your belly soft or pulled in tight, constricted? Are you holding your breath, holding yourself still so as not to disrupt or be noticed? Check in with what other indicators show up on your personal body dashboard – there are so many.

As we talked about in Chapter 1, the cultural narrative that we live with and live in is that to be human is to be divided and, in that division, the smart head is in charge of the burdensome body. We spend so much time up in that head that we are largely disconnected from our bodies unless they are "causing problems" or shouting at us in some way... Hungry! Hurting! Many of us have dulled and muted our ability to tune into non-cognitive intelligence within us (and outside of us), and what lies beneath the surface we simply forget about. We are so fast-tracked and busy we have lost some of our understanding of those other ways of being, lost touch with the fluidity and flow of our own energies. It's right there, though, ready to be remembered. There is even a name for it: interoception. It is the ability to perceive and interpret internal bodily sensations like hunger, thirst, tension, or emotional changes, and it is essential to helping you understand what is happening within, emotionally and physically. Every sensation in your body is a form of thinking that offers great intel on what's true for you, and when you know how you feel, you can work out what you need.

It is interoception that allows you to notice and process signals from your internal organs, muscles, and other bodily systems like the cardiovascular system – what does that racing heart want you to notice? Or the digestive system – what does that full stomach want you to know? Interoception also plays a crucial role in recognising and understanding your emotional state, often through physiological cues like butterflies in the stomach, sweaty palms or shortness of breath when anxious, or feelings of heaviness in the heart when sad. As such, interoception is a critical part of your self-regulation and the ability to give yourself what you need when you need it – like the comfort of a deep breath when you feel stressed or actually moving outside to get some air when you feel drained after a long spell inside.

Your body's energy is a mirror to the state of your mind. If you feel jittery and unsettled in the body, restless and unable to attend to something, needing to fidget and move, then that is the energy you will also find in the mind. If your body feels congested and blocked, you may feel "stuck" in your thoughts and unable to get any flow. If your body feels calm and open, you will likely find your mind in equally steady energy.

Not everyone has a well-developed interoceptive awareness, though, and some people have learned to deliberately override it, including pain and stress signals – especially where they have a history of trauma and shutting down/being confused by internal sensations. Trauma is held by the body, and so inhabiting it can feel agitating and uneasy. What can you notice right now, what conversation is your body having with you – a gentle chat or an urgent appeal?

When you live in your head, what you are doing is withdrawing from the avalanche of sensations in your body, and you do that in the belief that you will think more clearly and therefore act more rationally if you ignore everything but your thoughts. Emotions lead us down the wrong path, contort us away from reason and "reality", we think. We are well-indoctrinated to the idea that only reason matters, and emotions and sensations will betray us (especially if they include things like agitation, anger, loneliness, or feelings of vulnerability). And so, we come out of relationship with our bodies and into relationship with our own thoughts, ideas, and rules – in fact, we spend most of the day being seduced by our own thoughts, or thinking about ourselves even when those thoughts are vigilant and negative.

Take Adeye, for example, who we met in Chapter 3 – so much of her energy went on coping. She was so unwilling to feel, emotionally and physically, that she could ignore her interoception until she became really sick. For many people in this place, self-medication becomes the only respite from a frazzled and frantic nervous system that cannot be heard.

This is often true of overperformers, particularly ones who ignore their embodied self and instead stay on a constant quest for *more information*, scanning for new data like a search beam, so they might predict and control what is going to happen next, know in advance, know for sure. They can't let anything as inconvenient as an internal physical or emotional need get in the way of that seemingly vital work that the mind is doing. It is a kind of survival technique, and useful in crisis or truly big moments, but it's no way to live, ex-communicated from all but thought.

I have worked with many athletes who start by wanting to work on an isolated part of their psychology – fear, for example – and they see it in the way that we might see some kind of skill-building; a mental activity that happens in the private container of their minds and doesn't really involve anything else. They tell me that they feel connected to their body, but they talk about it as a machine – "This bit is good; this bit needs repair" – and they talk about their emotional shutdown as strength, drive, or fire – a necessary part of performance. In these athletes, reconnection to the body is something more like a reward post-performance – a burger and a beach – before they start again.

Sometimes, you don't know what you need until you make space to feel it. Sometimes, the most regenerative act is to let go. You can respect what was and the contribution it made to getting you here, and still realise that it won't serve the future you want or the wholeness we all need.

Inspired by Philip Shepherd's work on radical wholeness, I asked some of these athletes to reintroduce themselves to their organic, intelligent bodies and see what they then felt about what they needed in order to perform in a regenerative way, and whether it really was a new skill.[55] I asked them to take all of their attention to what they could feel under their left heel. Then at the back of their knees. Then at their mid-back and behind their ears. I asked them to keep their attention in each place until it felt like that area *was them*. Lots of fidgeting and frowning was involved at first. Then, once they settled into attention and presence and started to let go to the exercise, I asked them to take their attention to their liver, the place where toxins are processed and energy is metabolised. Then the place where their anxiety sat in their gut. Then to their brain and the sheath surrounding it, and all the electrical impulses travelling underneath it. And finally, to their hard-working heart. I asked which places were most tired. I asked which places felt most distant and in need of care. I asked which places were overperforming. The simple exercise not only brought up quite a lot of calcified emotion in these athletes, but it changed their openness to all the ways they could start to shift *in favour of life*. Could this exercise be useful for you too? What does your hard-working heart want you to hear? Which places in your body feel most distant and in need of care?

It is in reconnecting to the subtle energies and intelligence of the body that we can disrupt patterns of stuckness or staleness, patterns that keep us in an overperforming rut. If we get curious and start to tune in to and recognise what we actually feel in the body, what energy and emotion is there, rather than assume and predict what we might be about to feel, and seek to control those feelings with vigilance, we can combine cognitive and rational intelligence with the sensory knowing – a powerful place to respond from.

The body is a gateway. The body is where you can cultivate safety and learn to trust yourself. It is where we recover our "senses" – like balance, both physical and emotional. One of the above athletes learned to recognise that if his shoe (cleat) did not feel balanced in the starting block at the start of a race, it was an indication that he was feeling unbalanced emotionally too and needed to recentre himself with a grounding breath, and give himself permission to "run straight and free".

Our bodies are always willing to talk to us about upcoming danger, in adrenalin prickles and upright hairs on the back of our necks or the inexplicable urge to look around when we are in the middle of talking to someone. Fear is an animated experience felt first in the body, and you probably recognise it when it is something out of the ordinary. But do you notice those signals in the ordinariness of your everyday too? Your own voice sounds different in your throat when you speak openly and authentically and when you hide your feelings. These are bodied ways of knowing, body intelligences that can re-enliven and add to our ability to perform differently. It is not about downplaying or diminishing thought, but about adding the body's intelligence too; becoming whole in our experience. The body is a wonderland of information, data, signalling, and guidance.

And yet, until recently, we have largely ignored the fact that there is an anatomical brain in the gut and pelvic area as well as in the head. Now, researchers like Jane Foster at McMaster University confirm that the gut biome and the brain are not part of two separate systems – they are two parts of the same system, linked by the incredible polyvagal system.[56] The vagus nerve, sometimes also called the wandering nerve because of the way it meanders through the body, is the main sensory highway of this system, brimming with information and intelligence and also transformative capabilities in terms of helping us *feel more like ourselves*. This is especially true for people who have experienced trauma and become accustomed to shutting down their experience of themselves, especially experiences of the body. Dr Stephen Porges's breakthrough work on polyvagal theory has helped us understand trauma and the nervous system so much better, and because of it we now know that it is possible to get stuck in "freeze" mode or become shut down and closed off from the body, but that there are multiple ways back too, all of which include coming back to the wisdom of the body in some way and reintegrating; reclaiming your life and your wholebeing as we explored in Chapter 3.[57]

The gut itself produces 95 per cent of the body's serotonin, something closely associated with how we are doing mentally and something that drops when we start to burn out. When you know even this one little fact, it starts to become impossible to think of good mental health as a "head-based" concern alone. The functioning of the gut–brain axis affects sleep, mood, and appetite. Gut bacteria – all of those microbes and viruses and fungi and protozoa – have a huge effect even on your personality and the expression of your genes. In fact, researcher Mark Lyte has actually shown that if you transfer the microbiota from one animal to another, you can transfer the behaviour too![58] We are live and organic and we change constantly – that's great news for people who have been feeling stuck and wanting to regenerate.

The body, especially the gut, is not a side story when it comes to mental health; gut bacteria affect how you interact with the very world around you. As we relate to the body, we relate to the world. It can be integrated, or it can be separated.

The Japanese word for belly is *"hara"*. *Hara* is seen as a place of consciousness and attunement, a place where you come home to yourself, in the present. A friend of mine, naturopathic fire chef Polly Baldwin, does an exercise before her workshops where she asks people to lay one hand on their belly and one hand on their heart, close down their eyes, and ask, "How do I feel?" And then, "What do I need?" It is asking *hara* first, because the body knows first. Maybe you can try that too?

As the late and great poet John O'Donohue said: "Our bodies know that they belong, it is our minds that make us so homeless."[59]

The Psychological Microbiome

We can see from these core four principles of regenerative performance – presence, moving between modes and speeds, reconnecting with your wild clocks and natural rhythms, and embodied intelligence – that diversity in the way we live is a massive, underrated superpower in regenerative performance. And we can see that the gut microbiome is of vital importance in our health and functioning, and that it also needs a lot of diversity to truly flourish. Hey, this diversity thing seems like a clue…

What if you imagined that you had a psychological microbiome? A psychological environment that needed you to "feed" with good stuff and carefully monitor the amount of junk inputs? And what if you thought about making sure that you offered your psychological microbiome a lot of diversity too, because you know that it would be equally vital to your health and functioning?

Your psychological microbiome would be a place that would be as diminished and made sluggish by ultra-processed thoughts and rotten old ideas, as the gut is diminished by ultra-processed food and rotten old junk food.

It would be a place where a mental diet that only had (sugar-coated) positivity and "can-do" attitudes and work styles might be just as inflammatory to our wholebeing as a soda and a glazed doughnut with sketchy blue sprinkles is to the gut.

Your psychological microbiome would suffer from a behavioural diet that was mostly push, rush, gain, and pain – it would be too bland and sometimes toxic for your psychological health. A behavioural diet that included you ignoring inconvenient feelings and masking them behind "I'll sleep when I am dead" attitudes would lessen your performance resilience and "immunity" in the way a diet of beige-only carbs and carcinogens would lower your gut immunity.

You are as organic in your psychology as you are in your body. You are what you eat, or consume, in both cases.

If you want to be a regenerative performer, a performer who doesn't have to extract from themselves until they are so depleted they cannot perform anymore, then why not try thinking about intentionally diversifying your "performance diet"? It will leave you in a position to regenerate, a position where you can renew.

Diversity and conformity are opposites, like width and narrowness are opposites. So, what will diversity in your psychological microbiome take? Where do you need more width and less narrowness in your behaviours? Where do you need more spice and less beige?

Can you notice some of the places of rigidity or stickiness in your "psychological diet" today, things that you don't think really work for you anymore? They might be things that you are pretty attached to and fixed-minded about – things about which you might say, "That's just the way I do it" (a dangerous phrase in terms of regenerative performance!).

Check out some of the following questions and ideas to get you thinking about what kind of diversity you have today in your own psychological microbiome:

- Who do you spend time with that "feeds" you psychologically? This can be the nourishment of challenge as well as the nourishment of support.
- Who and what drain your "psychological nutrients" and leaves you feeling empty, hungry, or flat?
- What kind of performance behaviour puts you in a psychological sugar coma (like working on something you love, but doing it until you are running on adrenalin and then hit a slump)?
- What kind of performance behaviours give you a hangover (doing something until you are woozy), make you bloated (taking on too much), or give you the shits (saying yes when you didn't want to)?
- Which experiences fill you up and which empty you?
- Do you have any unnecessary "performance parasites" and "mouldy ideas" about who you need to be and how you need to overperform to succeed in your psychological microbiome?
- How much of your psychological performance diet comes from small, local, personally planted, and seasonal inputs?

Diversity looks like mixing it up. Do you mix up those experiences that come with high-performance expectations (must do well) and those that come with low ones (cruising along here is fine)? Or experiences where you are central and out-front (I need to be visible and at my sparkly best) and ones where you are peripheral and you can enjoy the background? Do you seek out conversations that feel a little risky but important and also the ones that feel safe and easy?

There is so much you can do to make positive, healthy, kind inputs to your psychological microbiome. As with the gut, time to digest is important. For both your gut and your psychological microbiome, honouring sleep, including napping, is essential. So is the use of movement to support emotional processing through the body – whether it is Feldenkrais or cliff-diving or a stroll, movement benefits the processing of emotional energy and helps you regenerate. Experts like Dr Peter Levine developed a body-oriented approach to releasing trapped energy and restoring a sense of connection with the body called somatic experiencing, which helps people to move out of hyper-vigilance, or move beyond what I called "performer trauma" in Chapter 3.[60]

Your own techniques will be many more than I have been able to share with you here, but my strongest, warmest encouragement to you is to tune in and trust yourself. Reclaim yourself. This is your life, and these are your performances. Be here for them. Delight in them. Dive into your ecological identity and the wisdom within it. Your energy and spirit are *worth* regenerating.

FINAL WORD

It is my hope that by changing your narratives, your mentalities, and your behaviours away from overperforming and depleting yourself, by coming home to yourself and feeling more whole, you will also start to see that the stress and angst you face is the stress and strain the world faces too. These are collective, cultural problems, but the change starts with you, inside you.

Living from wholebeing is remembering who you were before the world told you who to be. Everything you need has always been inside you – the intelligence, the art, the intuition, the drive – and you have the choice to allow it to unfurl. Like the nymph before it becomes a dragonfly, you can come out from being "underwater" by choice, by following your instincts to find your full expression, your wholebeing.

If this book called you, these changes are likely already happening in you, behind the scenes and out of your personal news cycle. Incremental nudges in understanding. Rerouted motivation. A perceptual sharpening of your feelings and senses that shows you that it's not supposed to be like this. Now it's time for what has already changed to become visible to you, and time for you to act on those nudges.

Such patient, honest work on integrating the pieces of your life can make your future – our collective futures – much brighter than you think. It is in this shift, this honouring, that I hope wholeheartedly that you might live your Life. Reclaimed.

NOTES

Introduction

1   "Key workplace mental health statistics for 2024", MHFA England, available at: https://mhfaengland.org/mhfa-centre/blog/ Key-workplace-mental-health-statistics-for-2024/ (accessed August 2025); "The burnout report 2025", Mental Health UK, available at: www.mentalhealth-uk.org/burnout (accessed August 2025).

2   "The state of wellbeing at work report 2024", Employment Hero, 19 July 2024, available at: www.employmenthero.com/uk/resources/ the-state-of-wellbeing-at-work (accessed August 2025).

3   Nic Paton, "A third struggling with burnout just three months into 2025 – poll", Personnel Today, 24 March 2025, available at: www. personneltoday.com/hr/a-third-struggling-with-burnout-just-three-months-into-2025-poll (accessed August 2025).

4   "Average Brit feels stressed eight days a month", HR World, 1 September 2021, available at: www.thehrworld.co.uk/health-wellbeing/ average-brit-feels-stressed-eight-days-a-month (accessed August 2025).

Chapter 1

5   Mary Midgley, *The Myths We Live By* (Oxford: Routledge Classics, 2011).

6   "Deepak Chopra – Buddha at the Gas Pump Interview", Buddha at the Gas Pump, episode 201, 7 November 2013, available at: https://batgap.com/deepak-chopra/ (accessed October 2025).

7   Philippe Descola, *Beyond Nature and Culture* (Chicago: Chicago University Press, 2013).

8   Lynn Margulis, *Symbiotic Planet: A New Look at Evolution* (New York City: Basic Books, 1999).

9   Nate Hagens, "Bill Plotkin: 'Ecological Awakening: A Path Toward Holistic Adulthood'", Resilience, 22 October 2024, available at: www.resilience.org/stories/2024-10-22/bill-plotkin-ecological-awakening-a-path-toward-holistic-adulthood (accessed March 2025).

10 Rich Roll, "Dr. Vivek Murthy: The U.S. Surgeon General's final prescription for America", episode 884, available at: www.richroll.com/podcast/vivek-murthy-884/ (accessed January 2025).

11 "Surgeon General: Parents are at their wits' end. We can do better", *New York Times*, 28 August 2024, available at: www.nytimes.com/2024/08/28/opinion/surgeon-general-stress-parents.html (accessed February 2025).

12 John Warner, "Moving Away From 'Schoolishness' Towards 'Joyful Learning'", Engaged Education, 11 July 2024, available at: https://engagededucation.substack.com/p/moving-away-from-schoolishness-towards/comments (accessed March 2025).

13 Ryan Lloyd Haynes, Instagram, n.d., available at: www.instagram.com/reel/DFicDu-NJsA/?utm_source=ig_web_copy_link&igsh=MzRlODBiNWFlZA== (accessed February 2025).

Chapter 2

14 Emma Gannon, *The Multi-hyphen Method* (London: Hodder & Stoughton, 2018).

15 Sally Dickerson, Kate Sweeny, Megan Robbins, Lee Cohen, "Social-evaluative Threat", November 2020, available at: www.researchgate.net/publication/346873945_Social-Evaluative_Threat?_

tp=eyJjb250ZXh0Ijp7ImZpcnN0UGFnZSI6InByb2ZpbGUiLCJw
YWdlIjoicHJvZmlsZSJ9fQ (accessed February 2025).

16 Jonathan Haidt, *The Anxious Generation: How the great rewiring of
childhood is causing an epidemic of mental illness* (New York: Penguin
Press, 2025).

Chapter 3

17 Guangbo Qu et al., "Association between adverse childhood experiences
and sleep quality, emotional and behavioral problems and academic
achievement of children and adolescents", European Child &
Adolescent Psychiatry, 33(2), February 2024, pp 527–538, available at:
https://pmc.ncbi.nlm.nih.gov/articles/
PMC9985439/#:~:text=Children%20and%20adolescents%20with%20
ACE,for%20children%20with%20ACEs%20exposure (accessed
February 2025).

18 Gabor Maté with Daniel Maté, *The Myth of Normal: Trauma, Illness
& Healing in a Toxic Culture* (London: Vermilion, 2022).

19 Bessel van der Kolk, *The Body Keeps the Score: Brain, Mind, and Body
in the Healing of Trauma* (New York City: Penguin, 2014).

20 Thomas Hübl, *Healing Collective Trauma: A process for integrating our
intergenerational and cultural wounds* (Louisville: Sounds True, 2020).

21 "A Return to Wholeness with Dr. Gabor Maté", workshop on
Commune platform, available at www.onecommune.
com/a-return-to-wholeness-with-dr-gabor-mate (accessed Dec 2024).

Chapter 4

22 Joe Robinson, "Why a workaholic will die before an alcoholic", n.d.,
available at: www.worktolive.info/blog/
why-a-workaholic-will-die-before-an-alcoholic (accessed February
2025).

23 "Long working hours increasing deaths from heart disease and stroke:
WHO, ILO", World Health Organization, 17 May 2021, available at:
www.who.int/news/item/17-05-2021-long-working-hours-increasing-
deaths-from-heart-disease-and-stroke-who-ilo (accessed February 2025).

24 Robinson, "Why a workaholic will die before an alcoholic", op cit.

25 N Rajshekar and Christoph Zacharias, "Karoshi", IBS Case Development Center, 2003, available at: www.thecasecentre.org/products/view?id=21050 (accessed February 2025).

26 Tricia Hersey, *Rest Is Resistance: Free Yourself from Grind Culture and Reclaim your Life* (Eugene: Aster, 2024).

27 Dr Chatterjee, "Dr Gabor Maté: The 5 life lessons people learn too late, why we should stop trying to live longer & how curiosity leads to compassion", Feel Better Live More, 3 April 2024, available at: https://drchatterjee.com/dr-gabor-mate-the-5-life-lessons-people-learn-too-late-why-we-should-stop-trying-to-live-longer-how-curiosity-leads-to-compassion/ (accessed April 2024).

28 Martha C. Nussbaum, *The Monarchy of Fear: A Philosopher Looks at our Political Crisis* (Oxford: Oxford University Press, 2021).

29 Thich Nhat Hanh, *Peace Is Every Step: The Path of Mindfulness in Everyday Life* (London, Rider: 1991).

Chapter 5

30 Marcos Mendanha, *What Nobody Tells You About Burnout: Practical and controversial aspects* (2022).

31 Julia Samuel, "Grieving a living loss: Navigating life after a health diagnosis", 27 July 2024, available at: www.juliasamuel.co.uk/support-posts/grieving-a-living-loss-navigating-life-after-a-health-diagnosis (accessed January 2025).

32 "Rupture and Repair in Relationships – the Gottman method", The British Association of Anger Management, n.d., available at: www.angermanage.co.uk/rupture-and-repair-in-relationships-the-gottman-method/ (accessed June 2025).

33 Vanessa Machado de Oliveira, *Hospicing Modernity: Facing Humanity's Wrongs and the Implications for Social Activism* (Berkeley: North Atlantic Books, 2021).

34 Robert Frost, "A servant to servants" (1915): https://thepoetryhour.com/poems/a-servant-to-servants/ (accessed March 2025).

35 Brené Brown, "Stressed and Overwhelmed: 10 Learnings that Changed How I Think About Emotions", 21 November 2024, available at: https://brenebrown.com/articles/2024/11/21/stressed-and-overwhelmed/ (accessed December 2024).

Chapter 6

36 James Ford, "'At the Edge of the Roof': A Zen meditation on a Rumi poem", Unanswered Question, Substack, 4 May 2024, available at: https://jamesiford.substack.com/p/at-the-edge-of-the-roof (accessed October 2025).

37 Adrienne Maree Brown, *Loving Corrections* (Chico: AK Press, 2024).

38 "Kin-centric rewilding 2 – continuation of the conversation with Daniel Firth Griffith", Accidental gods, episode 273 – part 2, n.d., available at: https://accidentalgods.life/kin-centric-rewilding-2-bonus-continuation-of-the-conversation-with-daniel-firth-griffith/ (accessed February 2025).

Chapter 7

39 Raya Dunayevskaya, *Rosa Luxemburg, Women's Liberation, and Marx's Philosophy of Revolution* (New Jersey: Humanities Press, 1982).

40 Dr Gregory Cajete, *Look to the Mountain: An Ecology of Indigenous Education* (Kivaki Press, 1993).

41 Kae Tempest, *On Connection* (London: Faber & Faber, 2020).

Chapter 8

42 Jalal Al-Din Rumi, *The Soul of Rumi: A New Collection of Ecstatic Poems* (San Francisco: HarperOne, 2002; translated by Coleman Barks).

43 "Earthly reads: Prentis Hemphill on what it takes to heal", For the Wild, 25 March 2025, available at: https://forthewild.world/listen/earthly-reads-prentis-hemphill-on-what-it-takes-to-heal#:~:text=%E2%80%9CThere's%20finite%20resources.,eventually%20make%20ourselves%20suffer%20too.%E2%80%9D (accessed March 2025).

44 bell hooks, *All About Love: New Visions* (New York City: William Morrow, 2016).

45 Manda Scot, https://mandascott.co.uk/ (accessed November 2025).

46 Pope Francis, 'In Loving Memory of Pope Francis', Professor Paul A Ryan, St Theresa of Calcutta, 22 April 2925, available at: https://saintteresaofcalcutta.org.uk/1143-2/#:~:text=April%2022%2C%202025,Statement%20issued%20by%20Archbishop%20Bernard (access revised October 2025).

47 *Olympic Rules*, International Olympic Committee (Lausanne, 1949), available at: https://stillmed.olympic.org/Documents/Olympic%20Charter/Olympic_Charter_through_time/1949-Olympic_Charter.pdf (accessed September 2025).

48 Rick Rubin, *The Creative Act: A Way of Being* (Edinburgh: Canongate, 2025).

49 "Because it's there", Forbes, 29 October 2001, available at: www.forbes.com/global/2001/1029/060.html (accessed March 2025).

Chapter 9

50 Professor Megan Reitz and John Higgins, "Permission to pause: Rediscovering 'spaciousness' at work", 2025, available at: www.meganreitz.com/spaciousness (accessed June 2025).

51 Reitz and Higgins, "Permission to pause: Rediscovering 'spaciousness' at work", op cit.

52 Reitz and Higgins, "Permission to pause: Rediscovering 'spaciousness' at work", op cit.

53 David Farrier, "Wild Clocks", *Emergence Magazine,* 23 January 2025, available at: https://emergencemagazine.org/essay/wild-clocks/ (accessed February 2025).

54 Katherine May, *Wintering: The Power of Rest and Retreat in Difficult Times* (London: Rider, 2020).

55 Philip Shepherd, *Radical Wholeness: The Embodied Present and the Ordinary Grace of Being* (Berkeley: North Atlantic Books, 2017).

56 Jane A. Foster, Glen B. Baker, Serdar M. Dursun, "The relationship

between the gut microbiome-immune system-brain axis and major depressive disorder", *Frontiers in Neurology*, 28 September 2021, 12(721126), available at: https://pubmed.ncbi.nlm.nih.gov/34650506/ (accessed July 2025).

57 S. W. Porges, "The polyvagal theory: Neurophysiological foundations of emotions, attachment, communication, and self-regulation", W. W. Norton & Company, 2011, available at: https://psycnet.apa.org/record/2011-04659-000 (accessed July 2025).

58 Mark Lyte, "Microbial Endocrinology in the Microbiome-Gut-Brain Axis: How Bacterial Production and Utilization of Neurochemicals Influence Behavior", *PLOS Pathogens*, 9(11), 2013, available at: https://pmc.ncbi.nlm.nih.gov/articles/PMC3828163/ (accessed July 2025).

59 John O'Donohue, *Eternal Echoes: Exploring our hunger to belong* (New York City: Bantam, 2000).

60 Peter A. Levine, PhD, Ergos Institute, available at: www.somaticexperiencing.com/about-peter (accessed August 2025).

ACKNOWLEDGEMENTS

Sitting down to write a book is not a solitary process at all. Those images of an author locked away alone, bleeding at the keyboard, are fantasy. Many hands and voices go into a project like this. For example, the voices of my clients, colleagues and community who have been willing to share their stories about tough stuff, sometimes about the worst periods of their life during burnout and lost identity. Your names are changed in these pages, but I hope that you each know how deep my appreciation runs for the courage and grace you have shown in the journey out of overperformance.

Then there are the hands that hold the door open for you to be able to dedicate the time – my partners in Dark Peak Soul Ltd, Andre, Regine and Ab who took more weight and gave me space – I'm grateful. To Taryn who literally held the door open to her Hay Loft with a desk in it and a coffee machine – I'm grateful. To my literary agent Rory Scarfe at The Blair Partnership, and the brilliant Liz Gough and team at DK Red who held the door open formally and whole-heartedly for me to write another book – thank you for your belief in me.

And to my editor Julia Kellaway. Really, your plain-speaking partnership bolstered me throughout the process. Your warmth, curiosity and enthusiasm about regenerative performance particularly were enlivening for me as an author. You have made a huge difference to this book with such a light touch – thank you.

Finally, I want to acknowledge all of those people from all walks of life and corners of the globe who took a moment to share feedback and reach out to me after my last book and along the journey. Those little moments you share of putting something I've written or spoken about to the test in your life and getting a good result are priceless to me.

After all, we're all just walking each other home.

ABOUT THE AUTHOR

Dr Pippa Grange is a highly sought-after regenerative performance psychologist and culture coach, globally renowned for her transformative work with elite teams and individuals in both sport and business.

Born in Yorkshire, she later moved to Australia to pursue a doctorate in psychology, there establishing her reputation as a formidable culture coach advising national sports teams.

As Head of People and Team Development at the Football Association (FA), she worked closely with the England men's football team ahead of the World Cup in 2018. Under her guidance, their performance united the nation and showcased the joy of competing with less fear and ego – the core message of her 2020 book, *Fear Less*. Her pivotal role as the team's psychologist is currently being immortalized in the upcoming BBC drama *Dear England* – adapted from the hit Olivier Award-winning stage play – in which her character is being played by Jodie Whitaker.

Today, her practice weaves together ecopsychology and performance principles, to help groups and individuals not just succeed but sustain and thrive. Her time inside the inner sanctum with athletes, coaches, and performers has sculpted Pippa's perspective on the great value of keeping the soul in winning, and remembering, above all, just to be human.